Junior
Visual
Dictionary

Junior
Visual
Dictionary

Miles
Kelly

First published in 2007 by Miles Kelly Publishing Ltd
Harding's Barn, Bardfield End Green, Thaxted, Essex, CM6 3PX, UK

This edition printed in 2010

4 6 8 10 9 7 5 3

Editorial Director Belinda Gallagher

Art Director Jo Brewer

Editor Rosalind McGuire

Editorial Assistant Carly Blake

Designer Candice Bekir

Indexer Jane Parker

Production Manager Elizabeth Collins

Reprographics Anthony Cambray, Stephan Davis,
Liberty Newton, Ian Paulyn

Assets Manager Bethan Ellish

ISBN 978-1-84236-897-8

Printed in China

British Library Cataloguing-in-Publication Data
A catalogue record for this book is available from the British Library
All artworks are from the Miles Kelly Artwork Bank
Made with paper from a sustainable forest
www.mileskelly.net   info@mileskelly.net

www.factsforprojects.com

Self-publish your
children's book

buddingpress.co.uk

Contents

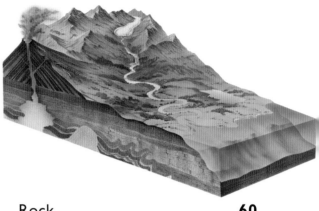

Planet Earth

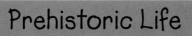

Prehistoric Life

Plants

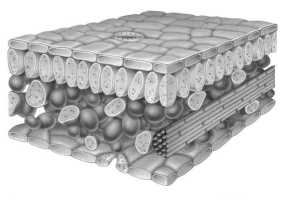

Animals

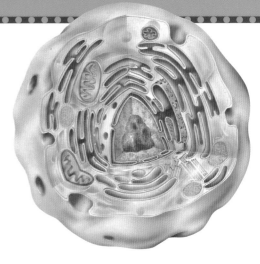

Human Body

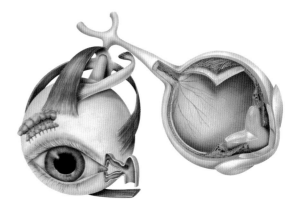

Transport

Universe

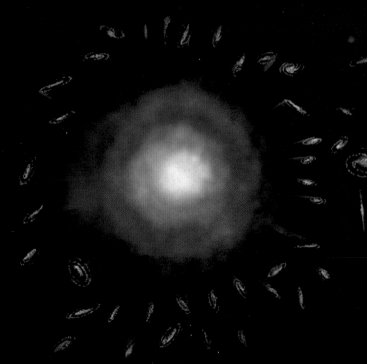

1. All the parts that make up the Universe were once packed tightly together. No one knows why the Universe started expanding with a Big Bang.

2. As everything moved apart in all directions, stars and galaxies started to form.

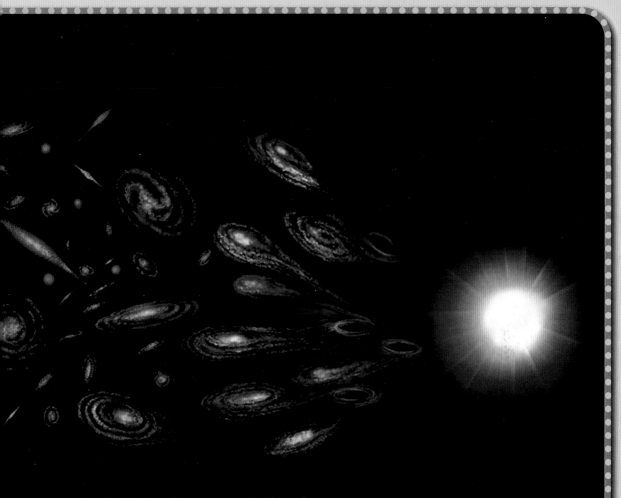

3. Today there are galaxies of different shapes and sizes, all moving apart. One day they may start moving towards each other.

4. The Universe could end as it began, all packed incredibly close together.

Stars

▶ **Birth of a star**

1. Clumps of gas in this nebula start to shrink into tight round balls that will become stars

2. The gas spirals round as it is pulled inward. Any gas and dust that is left over may form planets around the new star

3. Deep in its centre, the new star starts to make energy, but it is still hidden by the clouds of dust and gas

4. The dust and gas are blown away and we can see the star shining

▼ Death of a star

1. When a star runs out of gas, its middle parts shrink and its outer parts expand, making it much larger

Heavy stars end in a supernova – a huge explosion

Sometimes the remains of a heavy star fall in on itself to create a black hole

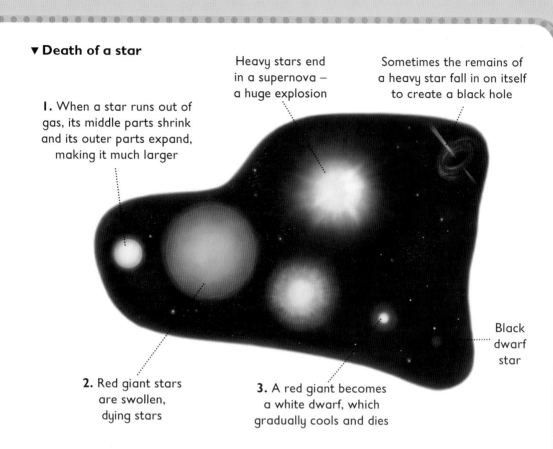

Black dwarf star

2. Red giant stars are swollen, dying stars

3. A red giant becomes a white dwarf, which gradually cools and dies

Big and small

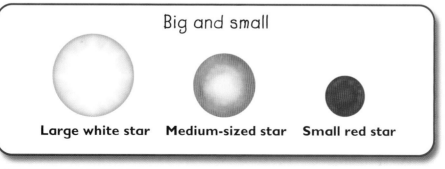

Large white star   **Medium-sized star**   **Small red star**

Galaxies

▼ **Milky Way**

Central bulge

▼ **Milky Way: side view**

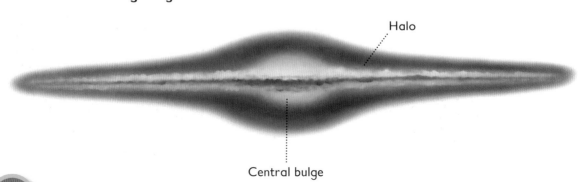

Halo

Central bulge

▼ Spiral

▼ Barred spiral

▼ Elliptical

▼ Irregular

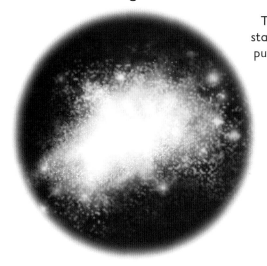

▼ Two galaxies colliding

Tails of
stars being
pulled out

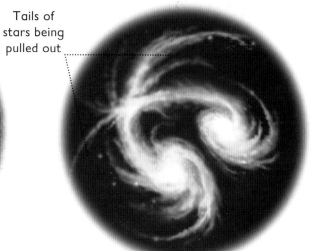

▼ Venus

▼ Mars

◀ Earth

▼ Mercury

▲ Pluto
Dwarf planet

► Jupiter

22

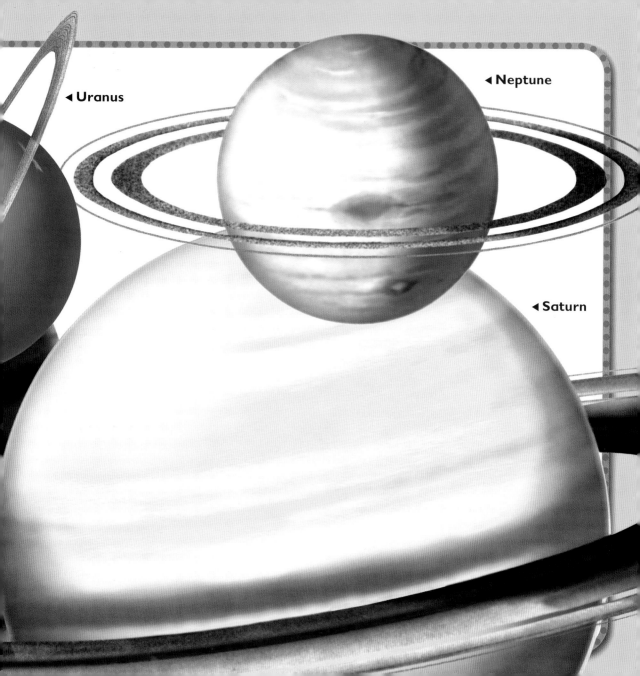

◀ Uranus

◀ Neptune

◀ Saturn

The Sun

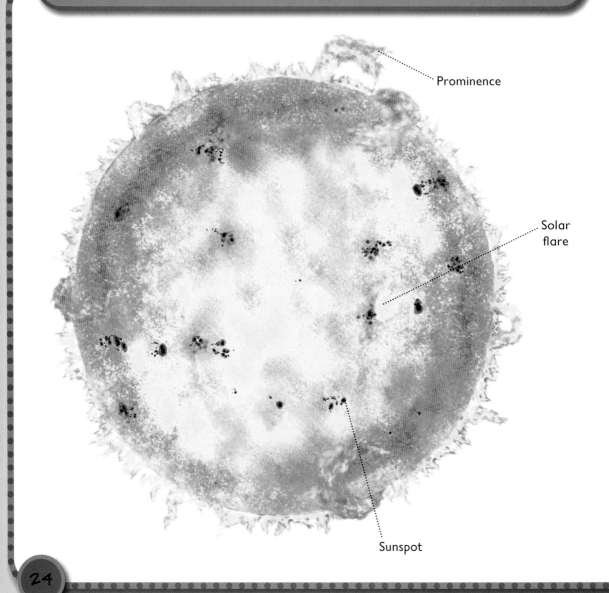

Prominence

Solar flare

Sunspot

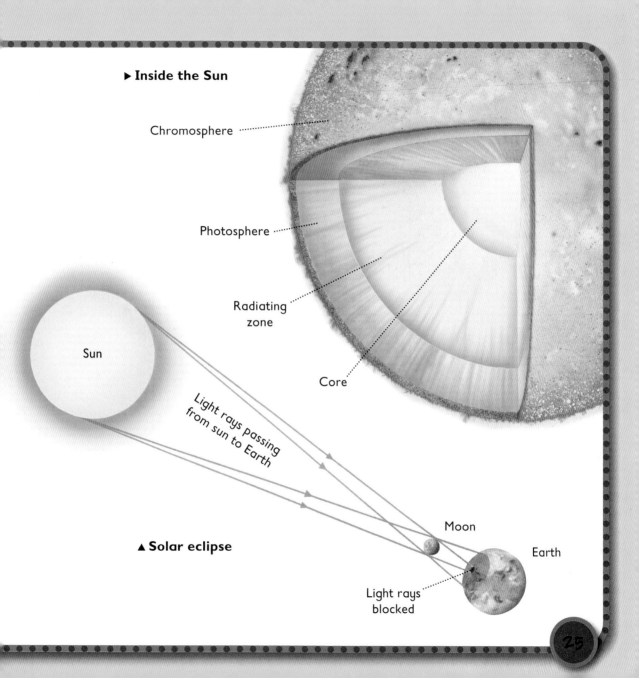

▶ **Inside the Sun**

Chromosphere

Photosphere

Radiating zone

Core

Sun

Light rays passing from sun to Earth

▲ **Solar eclipse**

Moon

Earth

Light rays blocked

25

Mercury

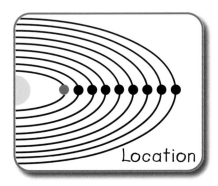

Location

▼ Surface

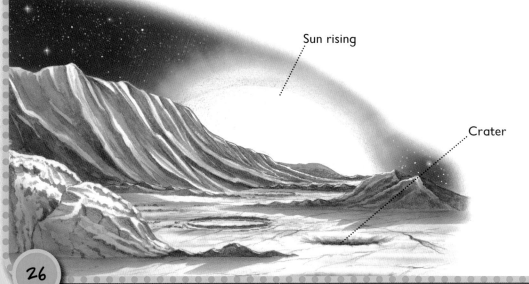

Sun rising

Crater

Venus

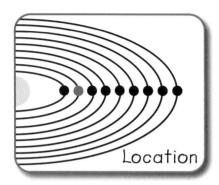
Location

▼ **Surface**

Volcano

Earth

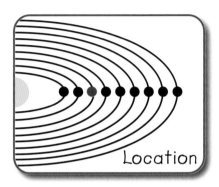

Location

▼ **Formation**

1. Clouds of dust and gas start to spin

2. Dust gathers into lumps of rock, which form a small planet

3. The Earth begins to cool and a hard shell forms

4. Volcanoes erupt, releasing gases, helping to form the first atmosphere

5. The Earth was made up of one large piece of land, now split into seven chunks known as continents

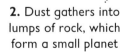

Mars

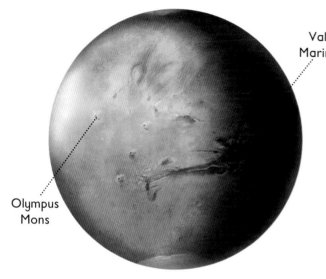

Valles Marineris

Olympus Mons

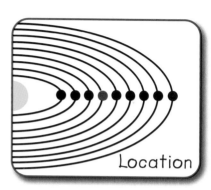

Location

▼ **Viking lander**

▼ **Roving vehicle** *Sojourner*

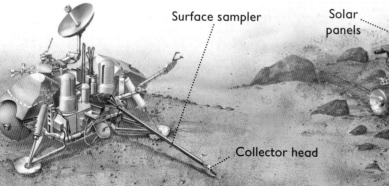

Surface sampler

Collector head

Solar panels

29

Jupiter

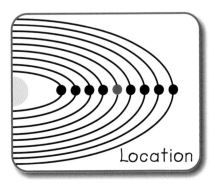

Location

Surface covered in clouds of ammonia

300-year-old storm, The Great Red Spot

Saturn

Location

▼ Rings

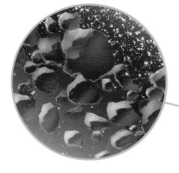

Chunks
of ice

▼ **Uranus**

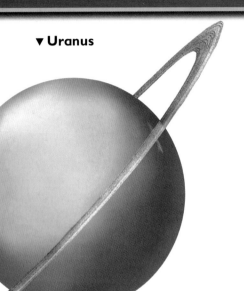

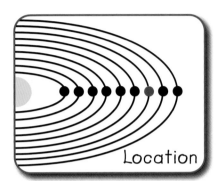

Location

▼ **Neptune**

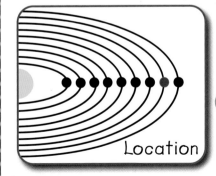

Location

Pluto, dwarf planet

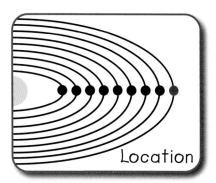

Location

Orbit of Neptune

Orbit of Pluto

Pluto's moon, Charon

▼ **Surface**

The Moon

▼ **Formation**

Earth was struck by a large object, and the fragments orbited Earth before clumping together to form the Moon

▼ **Surface**

34

▼ Phases

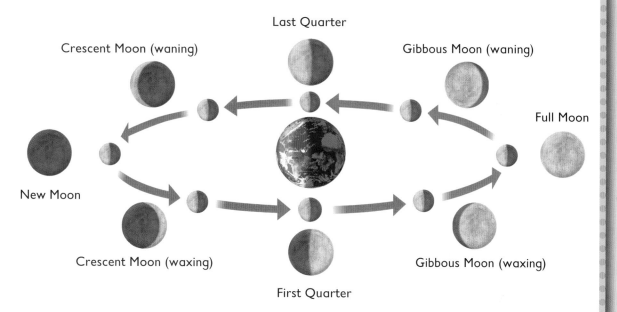

Last Quarter

Crescent Moon (waning)

Gibbous Moon (waning)

Full Moon

New Moon

Crescent Moon (waxing)

Gibbous Moon (waxing)

First Quarter

Other moons

Europa, one of Jupiter's moons

Ganymede, one of Jupiter's moons

Miranda, one of Uranus' moons

Comets, asteroids and meteors

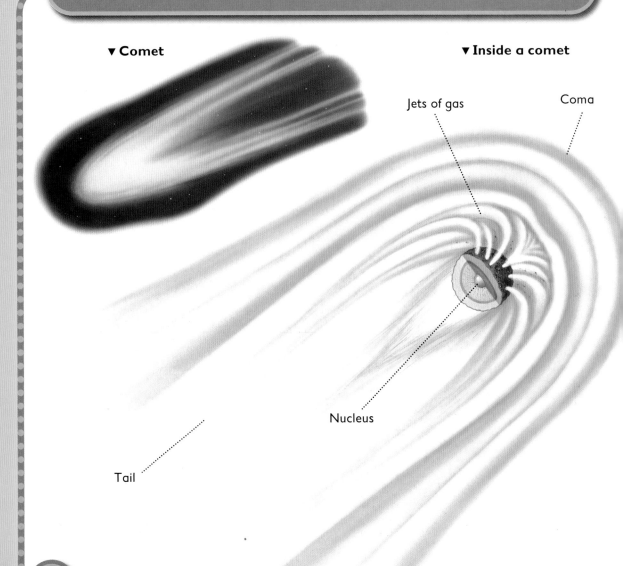

▼ Comet

▼ Inside a comet

Jets of gas

Coma

Nucleus

Tail

▼ Asteroid belt: location

Jupiter

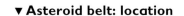

Mars

Large chunks of rock circle the Sun between Mars and Jupiter

▼ Meteors

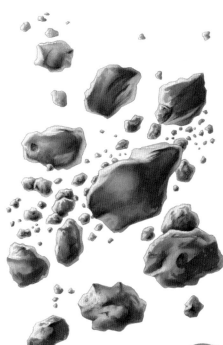

Telescopes and observatories

▼ **Observatory**

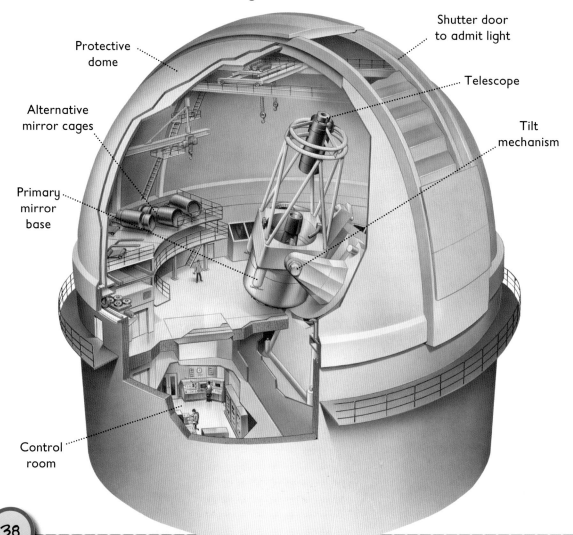

Protective dome

Shutter door to admit light

Telescope

Alternative mirror cages

Tilt mechanism

Primary mirror base

Control room

▼ Radio telescopes

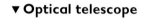

▼ Optical telescope

Main mirror to catch light
from distant objects

Platform for
observation

Secondary
mirror

Telescope moves around
to capture the best image

Axle tilts
telescope

Mount swings around

Constellations

▼ Northern Hemisphere

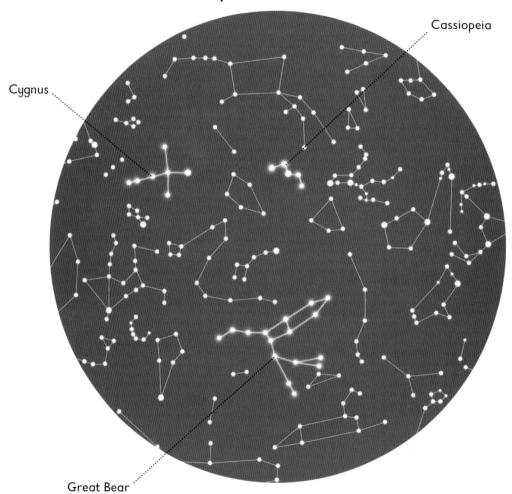

Cassiopeia

Cygnus

Great Bear

▼ Southern Hemisphere

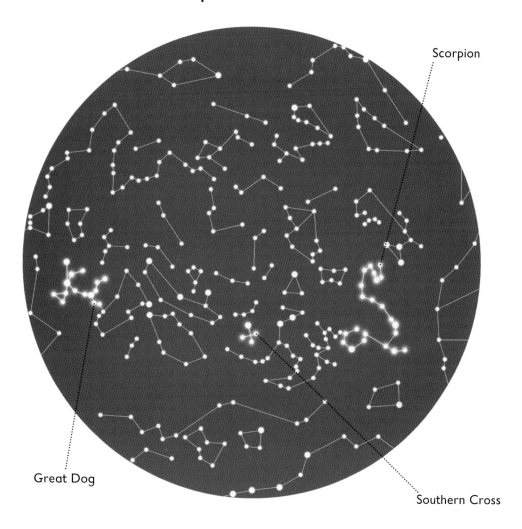

Scorpion

Great Dog

Southern Cross

Signs of the zodiac

▲ Capricorn

▲ Aquarius

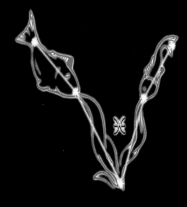

▲ Pisces

▲ Aries

▲ Taurus

▲ Gemini

▲ Cancer

▲ Leo

▲ Virgo

▲ Libra

▲ Scorpio

▲ Sagittarius

Probes

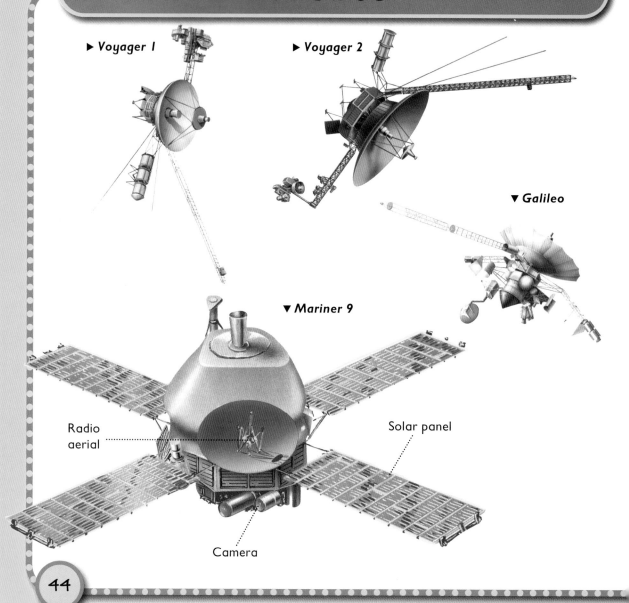

▶ *Voyager 1*

▶ *Voyager 2*

▼ *Galileo*

▼ *Mariner 9*

Radio aerial

Solar panel

Camera

Satellites

▲ Weather satellite

▶ Satellite
telescope

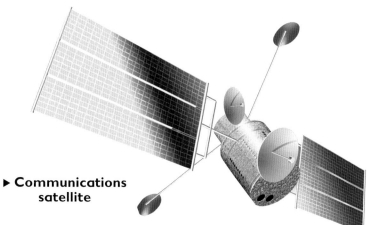

▶ Communications
satellite

Apollo spacecraft

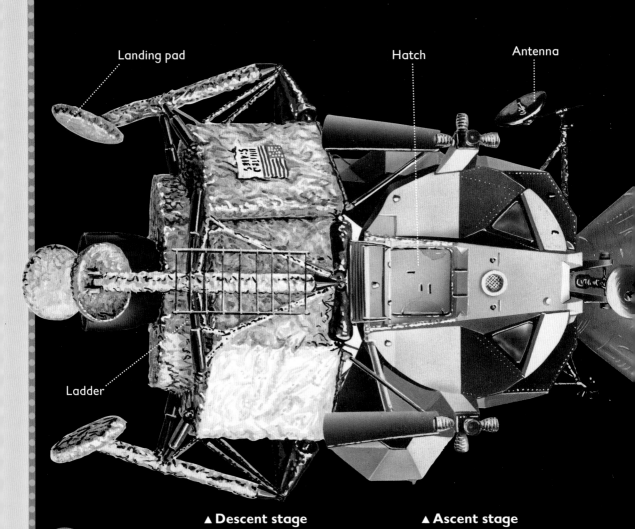

Landing pad

Hatch

Antenna

Ladder

▲ **Descent stage**

▲ **Ascent stage**

Thruster

Rocket

▲ Command module

▲ Rocket engine

47

Shuttles

▼ Shuttle flight

3. Main fuel tank falls away 130 kilometres up

4. Shuttle goes into orbit around the Earth

5. Shuttle crew place satellite in space

2. Solid fuel rocket burners fall away 45 kilometres up

6. Shuttle positions itself to re-enter the Earth's atmosphere

1. Shuttle blasts off using its own engines and two solid rocket boosters

7. Shuttle lands like a glider

▼ Landing

► *Columbia*

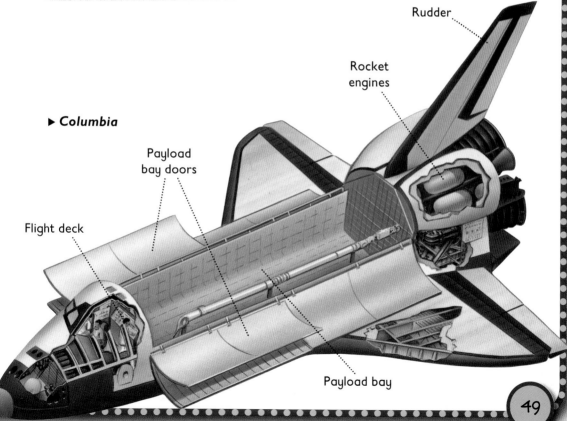

Rudder

Rocket engines

Payload bay doors

Flight deck

Payload bay

International Space Station

KEY

1. Solar panels for power
2. Docking port
3. Space shuttle
4. Control module
5. Living module
6. Soyuz ferry

Spacesuit

▼ Inside a spacesuit

Outer layers
protect from heat

Inner layer seals
the suit from the
vacuum of space

Layers inside a spacesuit

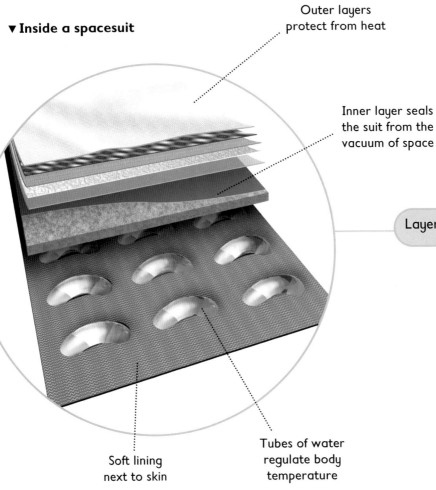

Soft lining
next to skin

Tubes of water
regulate body
temperature

Spacesuit

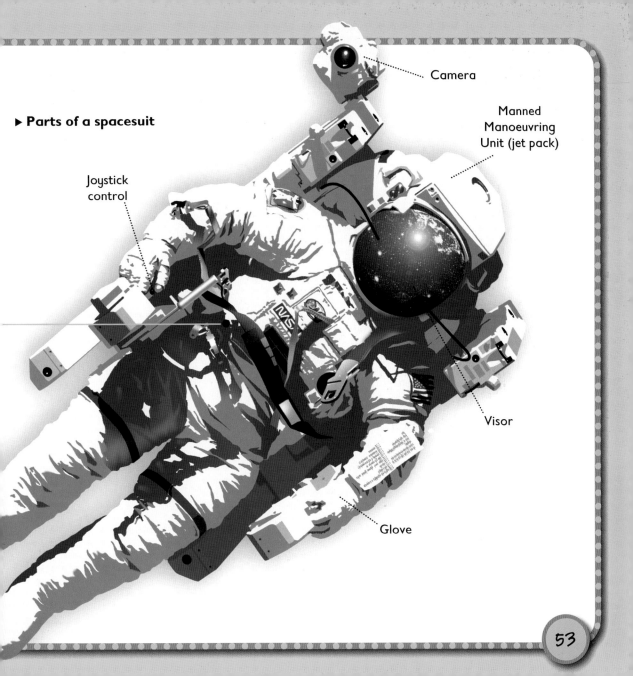

▶ Parts of a spacesuit

Camera

Manned Manoeuvring Unit (jet pack)

Joystick control

Visor

Glove

Planet Earth

The Earth

▼ Western Hemisphere

NORTH
AMERICA

SOUTH
AMERICA

▼ North Pole

▼ Eastern Hemisphere

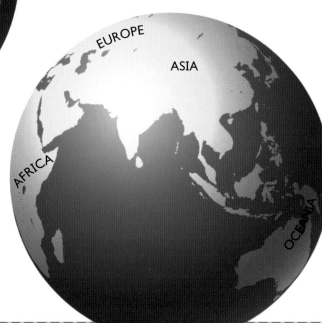

EUROPE

ASIA

AFRICA

OCEANIA

▼ South Pole

Earth's rotation

▼ **24-hour cycle**

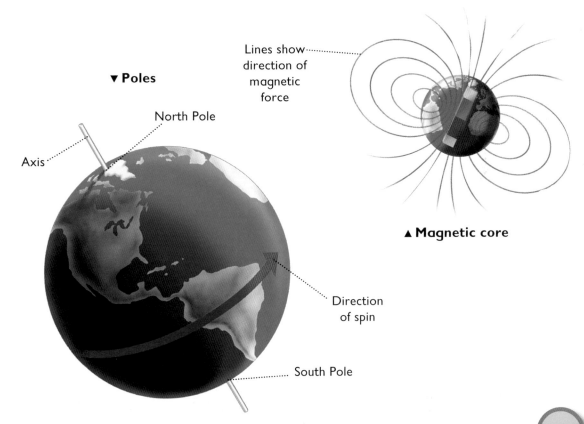

Lines show direction of magnetic force

▼ **Poles**

North Pole

Axis

Direction of spin

South Pole

▲ **Magnetic core**

Continental drift

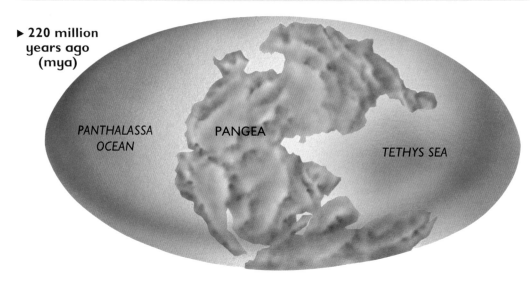

▶ 220 million years ago (mya)

PANTHALASSA OCEAN

PANGEA

TETHYS SEA

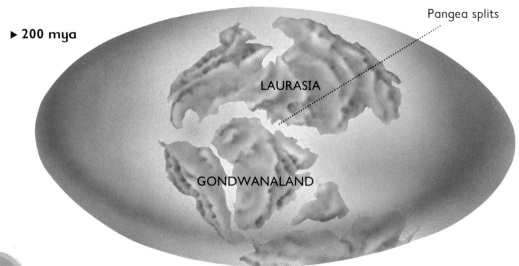

▶ 200 mya

Pangea splits

LAURASIA

GONDWANALAND

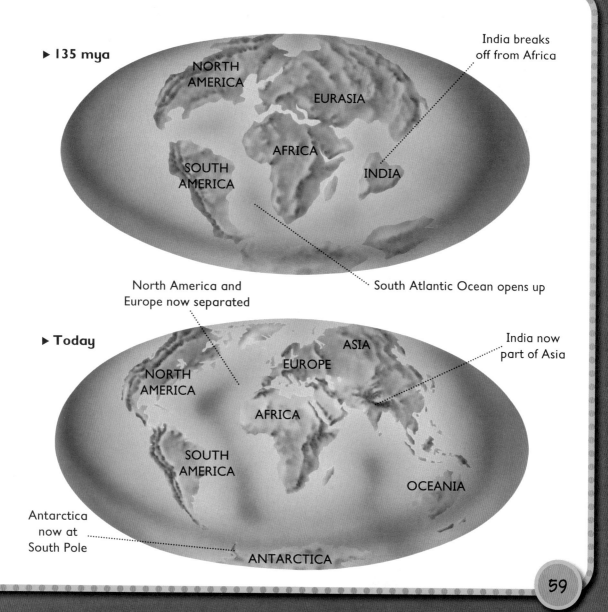

▶ 135 mya

NORTH AMERICA

EURASIA

AFRICA

SOUTH AMERICA

INDIA

India breaks off from Africa

South Atlantic Ocean opens up

North America and Europe now separated

▶ Today

ASIA

EUROPE

NORTH AMERICA

AFRICA

India now part of Asia

SOUTH AMERICA

OCEANIA

Antarctica now at South Pole

ANTARCTICA

Rock

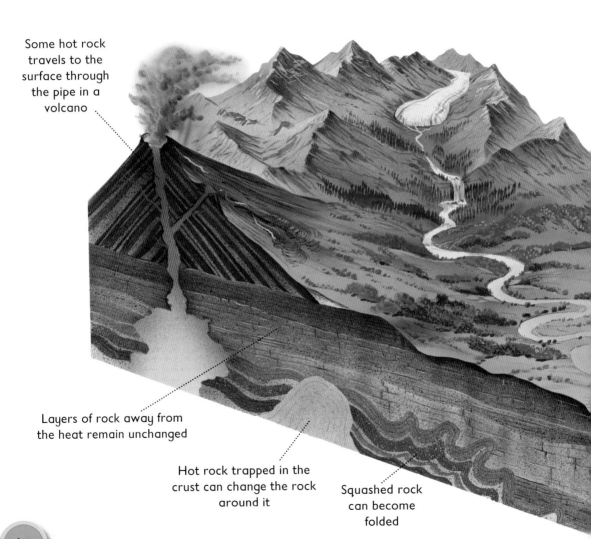

Some hot rock travels to the surface through the pipe in a volcano

Layers of rock away from the heat remain unchanged

Hot rock trapped in the crust can change the rock around it

Squashed rock can become folded

Earth's chemistry

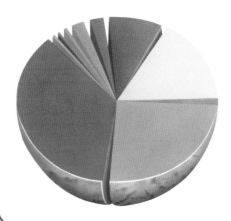

Element	Percentage
Iron	35.0
Oxygen	28.0
Magnesium	17.0
Silicon	13.0
Nickel	2.7
Sulphur	2.7
Calcium	0.6
Other	0.6
Aluminium	0.4

Rocks dip down away
from the coast to
make the deep ocean

Layers of rock
beneath the sea

Erosion

▼ **A tree root pushing its way through rock**

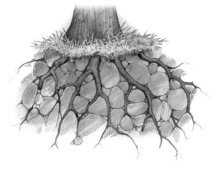

▼ **Flakes of rock break off unevenly, making patterns of ridges on the surface**

▶ **Sand-carrying wind carves away parts of rock**

Smooth rock face

Arch

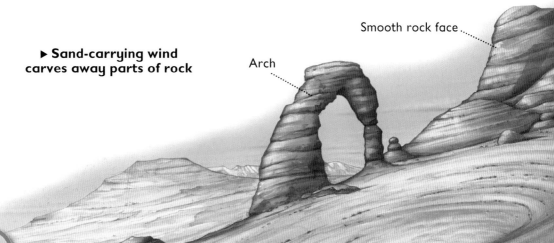

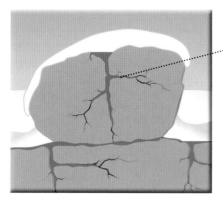

Water seeps into cracks, then freezes and expands, forcing the rock apart

▲ Frost-wedging

▲ Pressure from waves causes caves or arches to form in rock

▲ Uneven shape caused by expansion and contraction of rock due to changes in temperature

▲ Loose soil washed or blown away when forests are cut down

Types of rock

▲ Breccia

▲ Mudstone

▲ Gabbro

▲ Sandstone

▲ Chalk

▲ Syenite

Glaciers

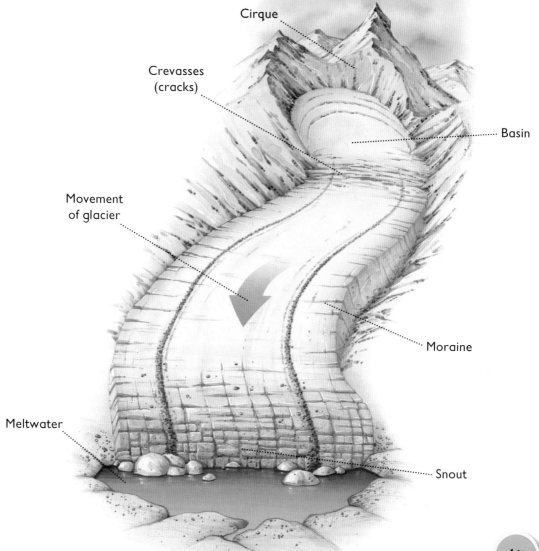

Cirque

Crevasses (cracks)

Basin

Movement of glacier

Moraine

Meltwater

Snout

Minerals

▲ Quartz

▲ Pyrite

▲ Gypsum

▲ Galena

▲ Calcite

▲ Barite

▲ Zircon

Hardness scale

Soft

Talc

Gypsum

Calcite

Fluorite

Apatite

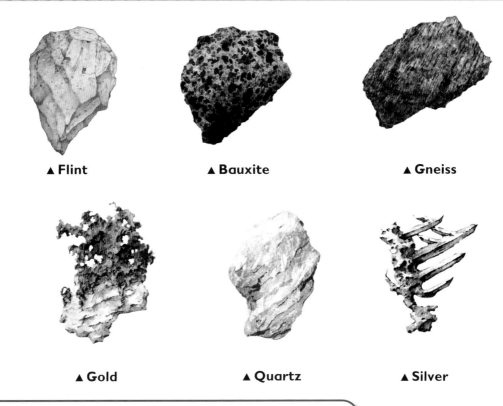

▲ Flint   ▲ Bauxite   ▲ Gneiss

▲ Gold   ▲ Quartz   ▲ Silver

Hard

Orthoclase   Quartz   Topaz   Corundum   Diamond

Gemstones

▼ Garnet

▲ Topaz

▲ Aquamarine

▲ Turquoise

▲ Amethyst

▲ Peridot

▲ Diamond

▼ Ruby

▲ Pearl

▼ Amber

▼ Opal

▲ Beryl

▼ Sapphire

▲ Emerald

Volcanoes

KEY

1. Main vent
2. Clouds of ash, steam and smoke
3. Lava flowing away from vent
4. Side vent
5. Magma chamber
6. Layers of rock from previous eruptions

◄ Shield volcano

▶ Crater volcano

◄ Cone-shaped volcano

Earthquakes

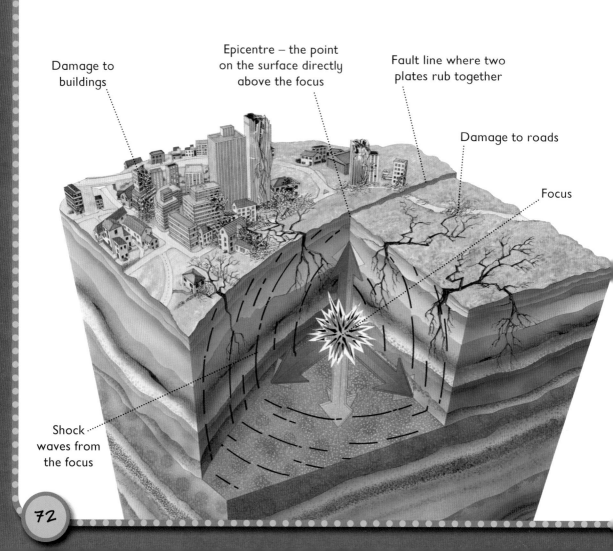

Damage to buildings

Epicentre – the point on the surface directly above the focus

Fault line where two plates rub together

Damage to roads

Focus

Shock waves from the focus

▼ Tsunamis

Direction
of pulse

1. A shift in the
seabed sends out
a pulse of water

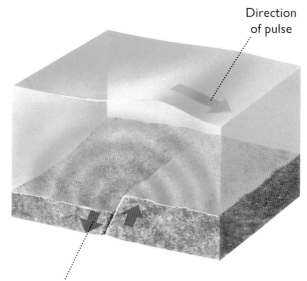

Direction of seabed
plate movement

2. As the pulse moves
into shallow water it
rears into a giant wave

Mountain formation

▼ Fold mountain

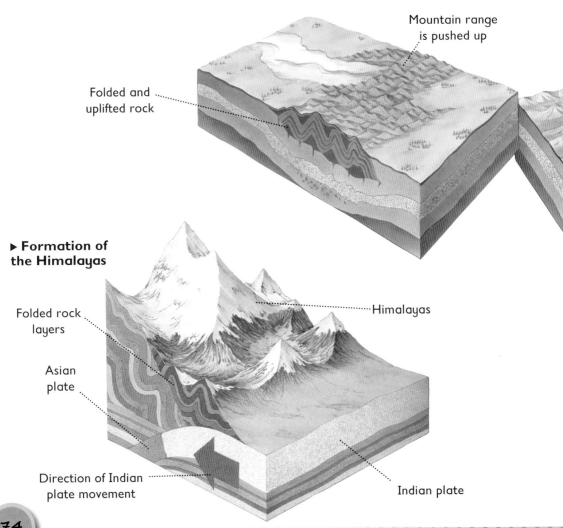

Mountain range
is pushed up

Folded and
uplifted rock

**▶ Formation of
the Himalayas**

Folded rock
layers

Asian
plate

Himalayas

Direction of Indian
plate movement

Indian plate

▼ Volcanic mountain

▼ Block mountain

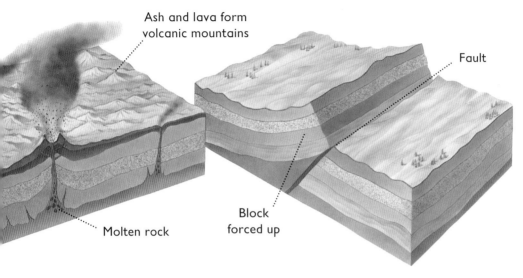

Ash and lava form
volcanic mountains

Molten rock

Fault

Block
forced up

Mountain high

The highest mountains in each
continent, to scale

Jayakusuma
(Oceania)

Elbrus
(Europe)

Kilimanjaro
(Africa)

**Mount
Mckinley**
(North America)

Aconcagua
(South America)

**Mount
Everest**
(Asia)

Oceans

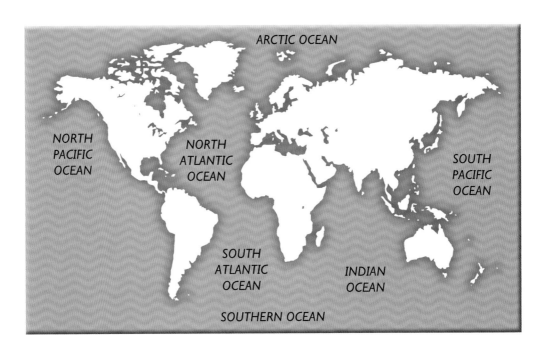

ARCTIC OCEAN

NORTH
PACIFIC
OCEAN

NORTH
ATLANTIC
OCEAN

SOUTH
PACIFIC
OCEAN

SOUTH
ATLANTIC
OCEAN

INDIAN
OCEAN

SOUTHERN OCEAN

▼ Tides

1. The sea moves upwards and inland as the tide rises

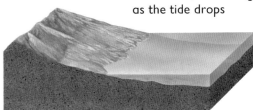

2. The sea ebbs, retreating as the tide drops

▶ Currents

Surface currents

Underwater currents

Wave movement

▼ Coastline

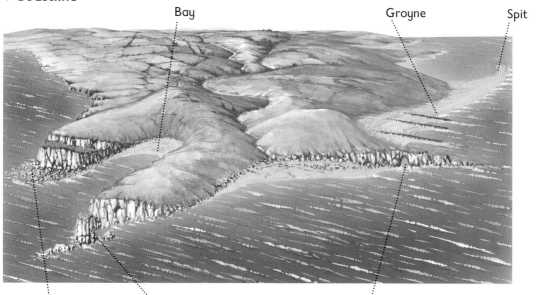

Bay

Groyne

Spit

Wave-cut platform

Sea stack

Arch

Islands

▼ Island formation

Volcano erupting on the seabed – molten rock breaks through the Earth's crust

▼ Atoll formation

1. Coral starts to grow

2. Lagoon appears around volcano

As more lava is deposited on the seabed, a cone shape builds up

The lava breaks the water's surface, forming a new island

3. Volcano disappears

4. Coral atoll is left behind

Rock pool

KEY

1 Limpet
2 Blenny fish
3 Shrimp
4 Anemone
5 Starfish
6 Crab
7 Hermit crab
8 Razor shell
9 Mussel

81

Rivers

▼ Course

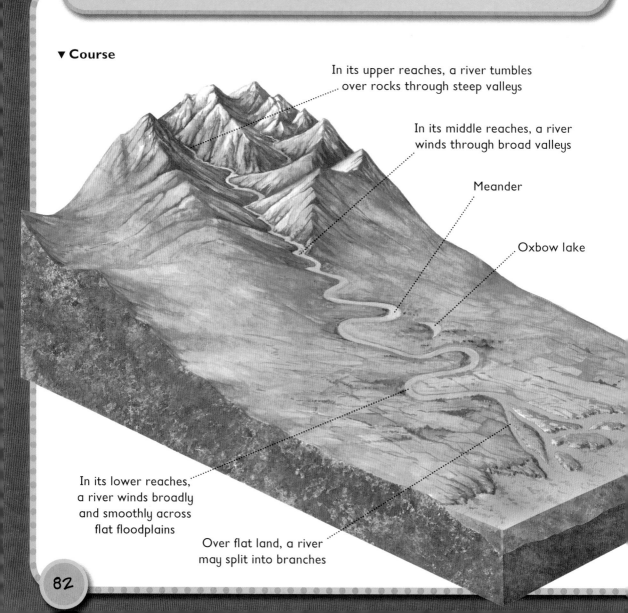

In its upper reaches, a river tumbles over rocks through steep valleys

In its middle reaches, a river winds through broad valleys

Meander

Oxbow lake

In its lower reaches, a river winds broadly and smoothly across flat floodplains

Over flat land, a river may split into branches

Lakes

▼ Formation

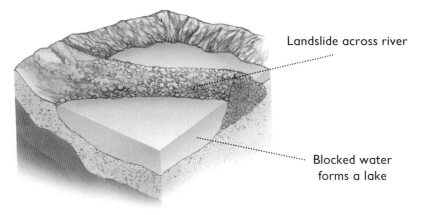

Landslide across river

Blocked water forms a lake

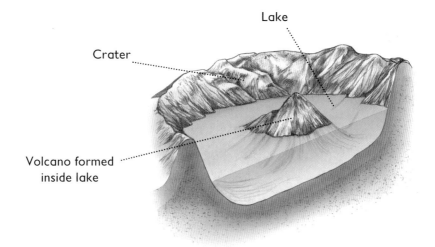

Lake

Crater

Volcano formed inside lake

Caves

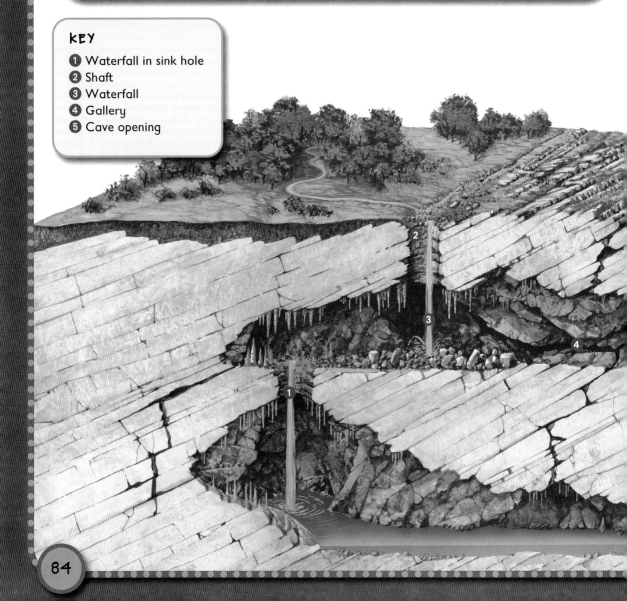

KEY
1 Waterfall in sink hole
2 Shaft
3 Waterfall
4 Gallery
5 Cave opening

► Formation

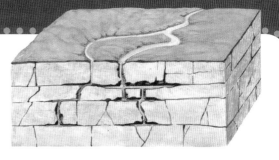

1. Water seeps through cracks in rock

2. Underground stream carves into rock

3. Large cave system develops

⑤

Atmosphere

KEY

1 Earth
2 Troposphere
3 Stratosphere
4 Mesosphere
5 Thermosphere
6 Exosphere

▶ **'Greenhouse' effect**

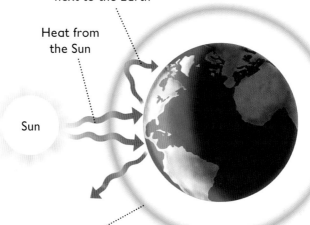

Heat trapped
next to the Earth

Heat from
the Sun

Sun

'Greenhouse' gases

▼ Pollution

Factories pump out chemicals that can cause acid rain

Cutting down trees can devastate forests and wildlife

Exhaust fumes from traffic clog up the atmosphere

Rubbish is dumped in rivers

Water cycle

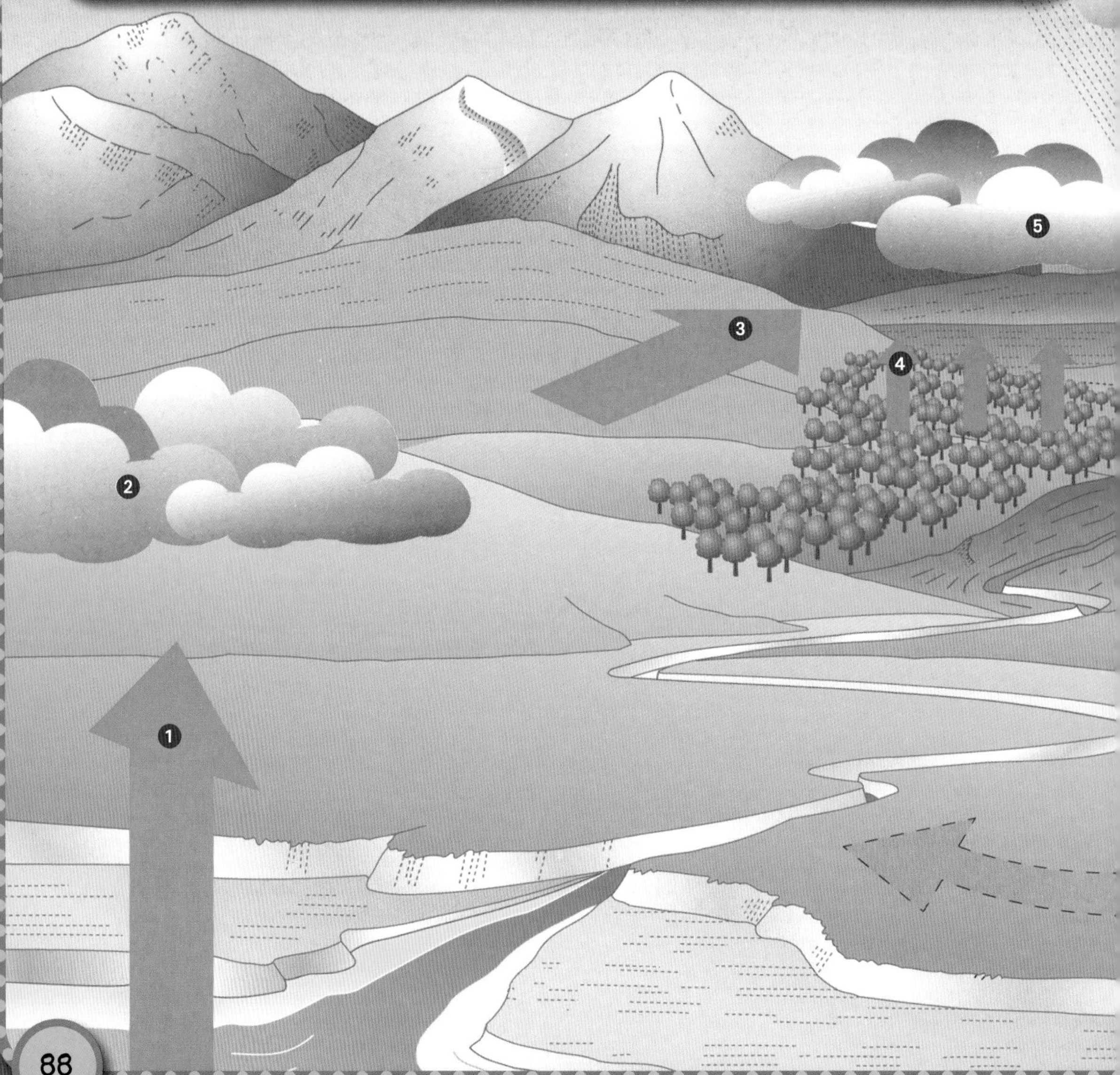

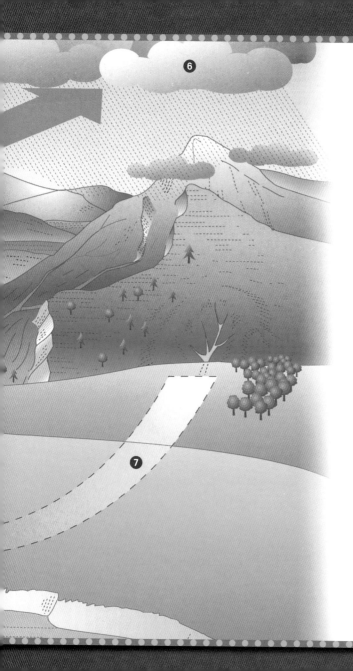

KEY

1. Water evaporates from the sea
2. Water vapour condenses to form clouds
3. Clouds rise
4. Water vapour is given off by forests
5. Clouds become larger and heavier as more water vapour sticks together
6. Clouds become too heavy – the water falls to Earth as rain
7. Rain falls into rivers, which run back to the sea

Clouds

Virga

Cumulonimbus

Cumulus

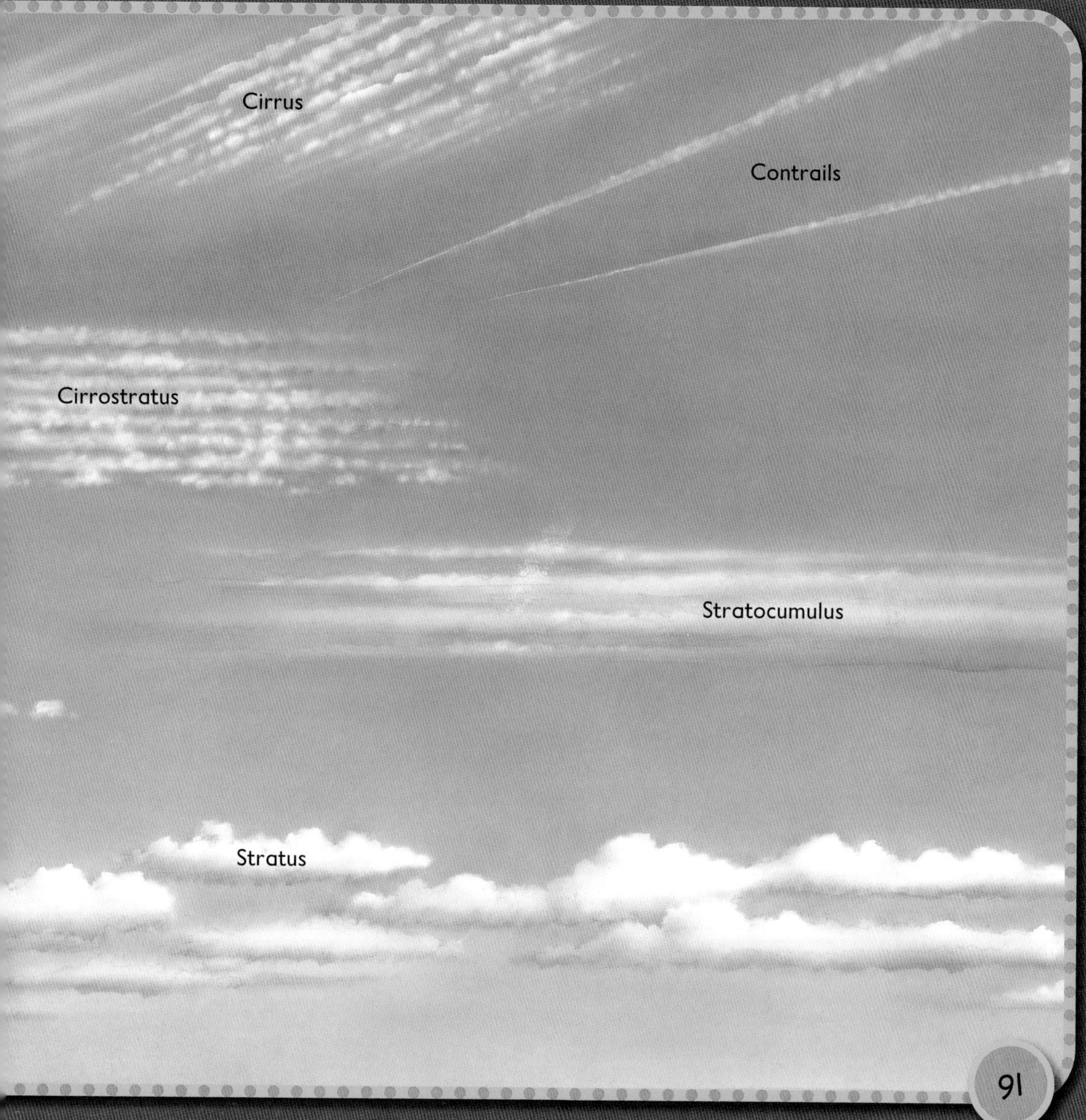

Cirrus

Contrails

Cirrostratus

Stratocumulus

Stratus

Wind

▼ **Pattern of the world's main winds**

North Pole

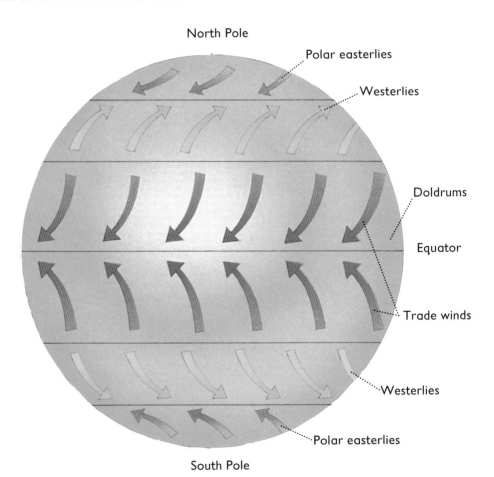

Polar easterlies

Westerlies

Doldrums

Equator

Trade winds

Westerlies

Polar easterlies

South Pole

▼ Beaufort Scale

Force 0: Calm

Force 1: Light air

Force 2: Light breeze

Force 3: Gentle breeze

Force 4: Moderate breeze

Force 5: Fresh breeze

Force 6: Strong breeze

Force 7: Near gale

Force 8: Gale

Force 9: Strong gale

Force 10: Storm

Force 11: Violent storm

Force 12: Hurricane

KEY

Warm front

Cold front

Occluded front:
a cold front meets
a warm front

Isobars: connect
places with the
same air pressure

Line: wind strength
Circle: cloud cover

Strong wind (three
lines on tail)

Area of calm with
lots of cloud cover

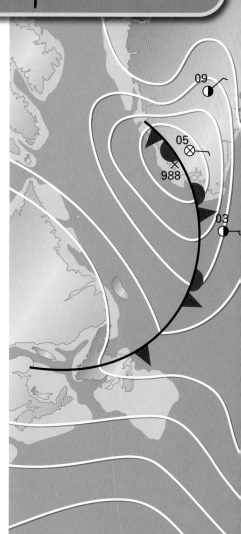

Climate

◄ Tropical grassland

◄ Tropical forest

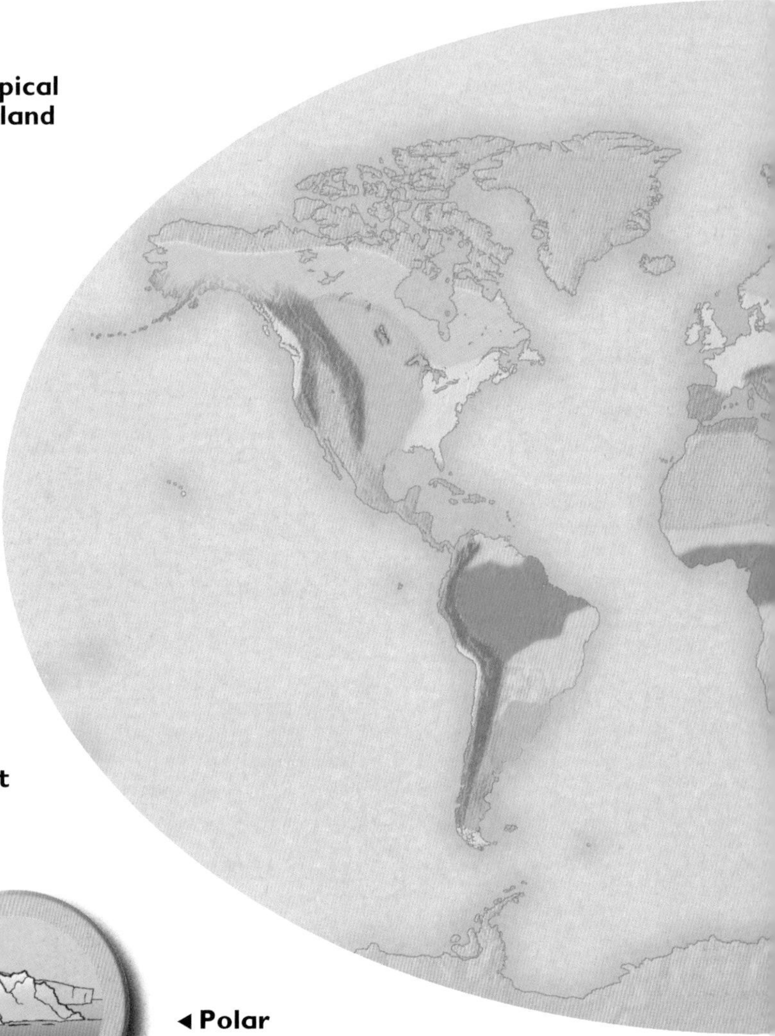

◄ Desert

◄ Polar

▶ **Mountainous**

▶ **Dry temperate**

▶ **Wet temperate**

▶ **Cold temperate**

▶ **Temperate grassland**

Northern spring

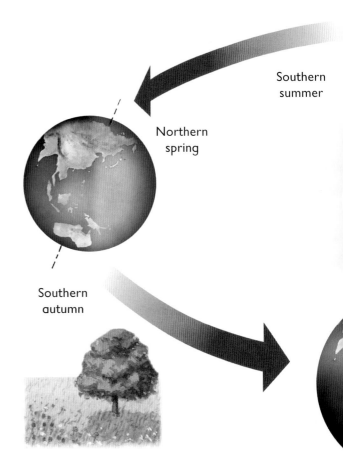

Southern summer

Northern spring

Southern autumn

Northern summer

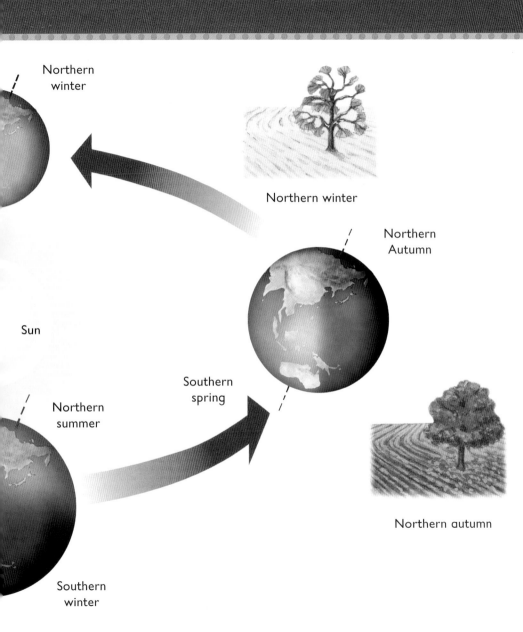

Northern
winter

Northern winter

Northern
Autumn

Sun

Southern
spring

Northern
summer

Northern autumn

Southern
winter

99

Prehistoric Life

Fossil formation

1. An animal (such as *Velociraptor* – shown here) dies, and its flesh and other soft body parts rot away or are eaten by other animals.

2. The bones and teeth are buried under layers of mud and sand.

3. Over millions of years, minerals replace the dinosaur bones, but preserve their shape and form.

4. If the rock containing the fossils gets lifted up and eroded, the fossils become exposed.

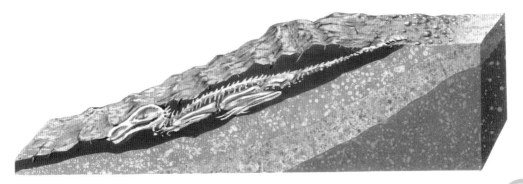

Early plants

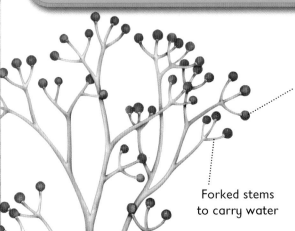

Spore-filled caps

Forked stems
to carry water

▲ *Cooksonia*

▼ *Archaefructus*

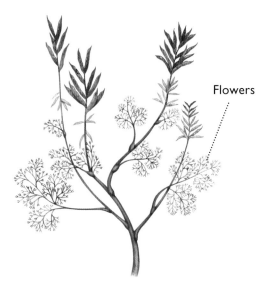

Flowers

◄ Lichen

104

▼ Stromatolites
Fossils of algae and bacteria

▲ *Lepidodendron*
Giant type of clubmoss

▼ Prehistoric landscape

Cycad

Tree fern

Early sea life

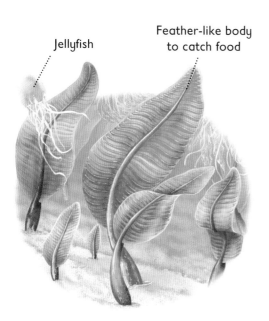

▼ *Charnia*
Early type of coral

Jellyfish

Feather-like body
to catch food

Protective
spiral shell

Soft
body

▲ **Ammonite**
Early shellfish

Long claws to
tear apart prey

► *Pterygotus*
Early sea scorpion

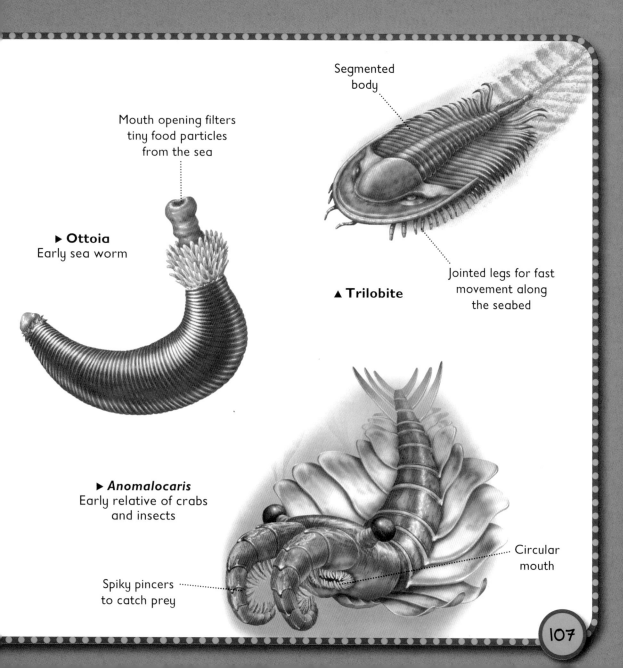

Mouth opening filters
tiny food particles
from the sea

▶ **Ottoia**
Early sea worm

Segmented
body

▲ **Trilobite**

Jointed legs for fast
movement along
the seabed

▶ *Anomalocaris*
Early relative of crabs
and insects

Circular
mouth

Spiky pincers
to catch prey

Prehistoric fish

▶ *Pikaia*

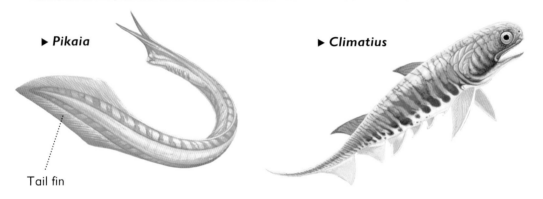

Tail fin

▶ *Climatius*

▼ *Hybodus*
Early shark

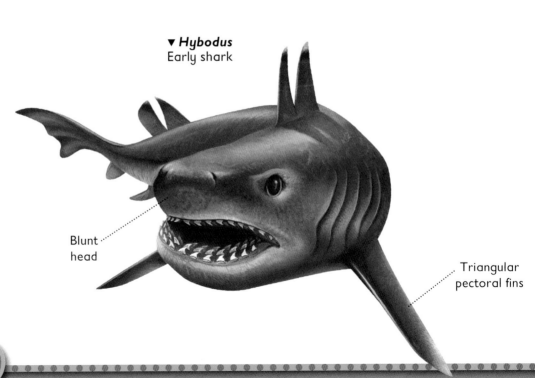

Blunt
head

Triangular
pectoral fins

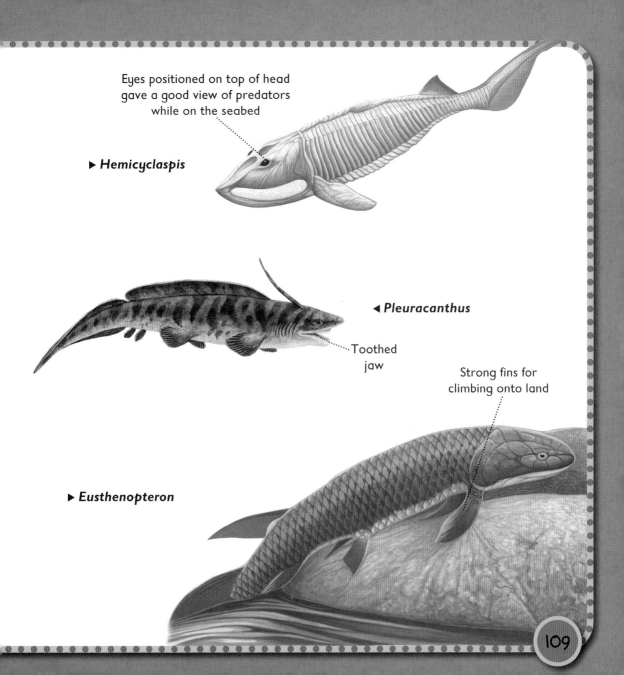

Eyes positioned on top of head
gave a good view of predators
while on the seabed

▶ *Hemicyclaspis*

◀ *Pleuracanthus*

Toothed
jaw

Strong fins for
climbing onto land

▶ *Eusthenopteron*

109

Prehistoric amphibians

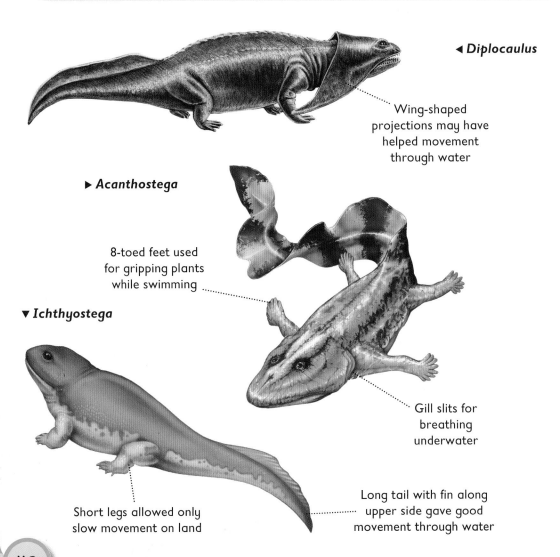

◄ *Diplocaulus*

Wing-shaped projections may have helped movement through water

► *Acanthostega*

8-toed feet used for gripping plants while swimming

▼ *Ichthyostega*

Gill slits for breathing underwater

Short legs allowed only slow movement on land

Long tail with fin along upper side gave good movement through water

Shortened
tail

Froglike
skull

▲ *Triadobatrachus*

▼ *Mastodonsaurus*

Eyes and nostrils
positioned on top
of the head allowed
Mastodonsaurus to
breathe and look
around while
underwater

Prehistoric reptiles

▶ *Hylonomus*

Tall sail-like fin regulated
body temperature

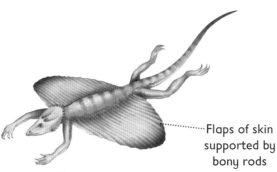

Dagger-like teeth

▲ *Dimetrodon*

▶ *Varanosaurus*

Flaps of skin
supported by
bony rods

▲ *Coelurosauravus*

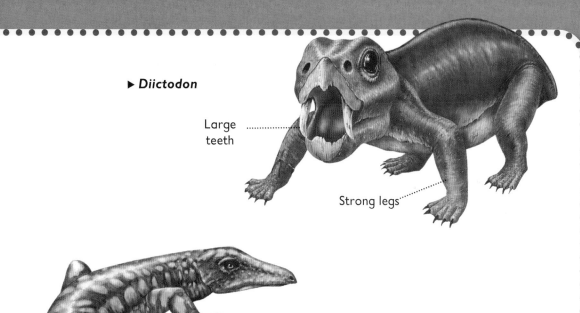

▶ *Diictodon*

Large
teeth ....

Strong legs ....

▲ *Chasmatosaurus*

▼ *Moschops*

Chisel-edged ....
teeth

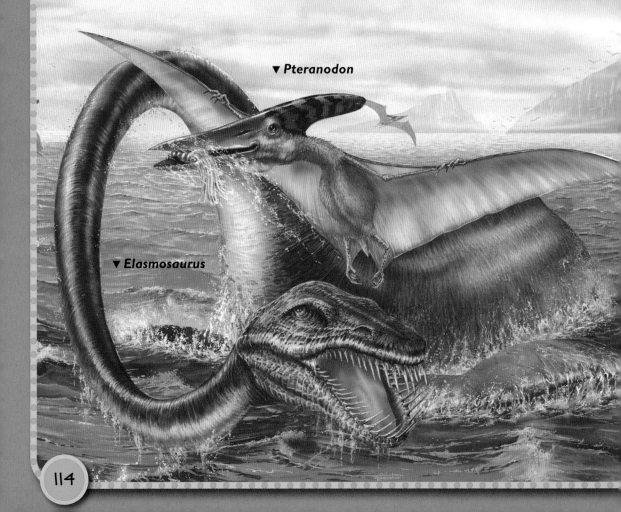

▼ Pteranodon

▼ Elasmosaurus

▼ *Archelon*

Powerful
front flippers

Fur-covered
body

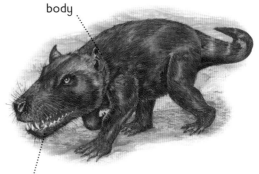

▲ *Cynognathus*

Strong jaws,
powerful
enough to bite
through bone

▼ *Protosuchus*

Long legs gave
speed on dry land
when hunting

Paddle-shaped
limbs

▲ *Mosasaurus*

Dinosaur hips

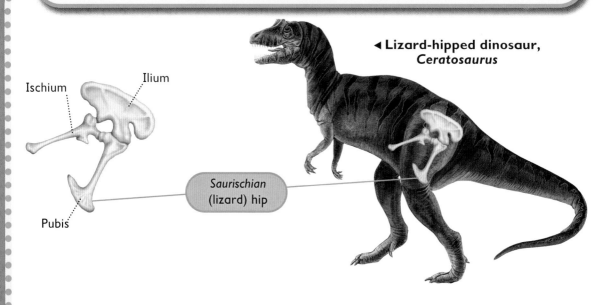

◀ **Lizard-hipped dinosaur,**
Ceratosaurus

Ischium

Ilium

Saurischian
(lizard) hip

Pubis

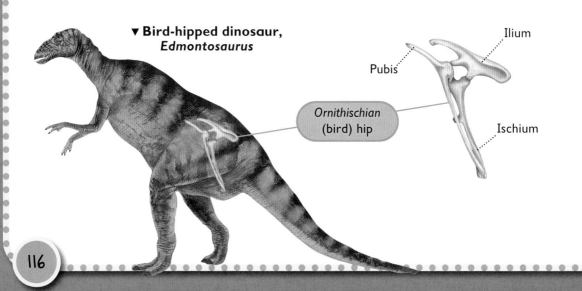

▼ **Bird-hipped dinosaur,**
Edmontosaurus

Ilium

Pubis

Ornithischian
(bird) hip

Ischium

Dinosaur bones

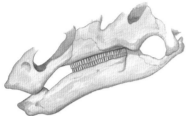

◀ *Edmontosaurus* skull

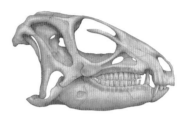

▲ *Heterodontosaurus* skull

▼ *Apatosaurus* skull

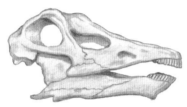

▶ *Mamenchisaurus* head and neck bones

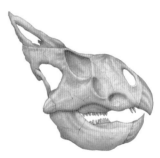

▲ *Protoceratops* skull

▶ *Plateosaurus* foot bones

▶ Foot and claw bones of a large, plant-eating dinosaur

▼ *Deinonychus* claws

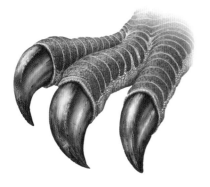

▼ *Baryonyx* thumb claw

▼ *Deinonychus*

Deinonychus probably leapt onto its prey to attack it

◄ *Maiasaura*

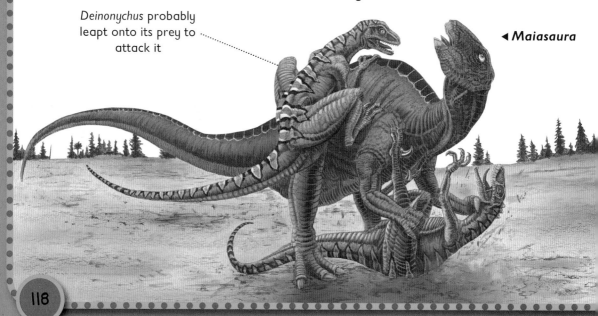

▼ *Tyrannosaurus Rex*

Eyes faced forward

Large nostrils indicate a good sense of smell

Teeth grew up to 30 cm in length

Defence

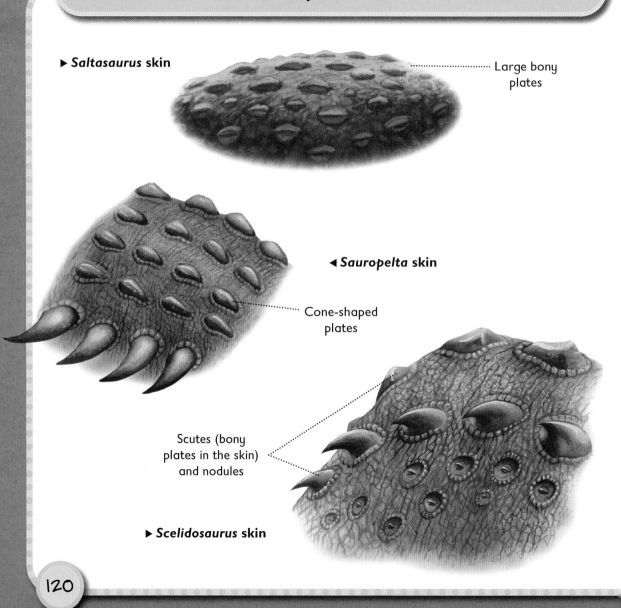

► *Saltasaurus* skin

Large bony plates

◄ *Sauropelta* skin

Cone-shaped plates

Scutes (bony plates in the skin) and nodules

► *Scelidosaurus* skin

Fused plates
of bone ....

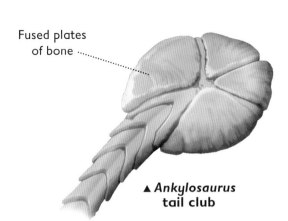

▲ *Ankylosaurus*
tail club

▼ *Shunosaurus* **tail
and tail club**

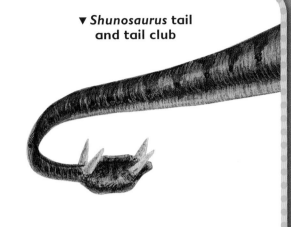

Ceratopsia

A group of dinosaurs with distinctive neck frills,
horned faces and parrot-like beaks

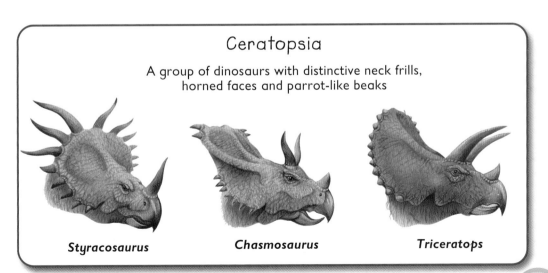

Styracosaurus   *Chasmosaurus*   *Triceratops*

Triassic dinosaurs 220–203 mya

▼ *Herrerasaurus*
(huh-RARE-uh-SAW-rus)

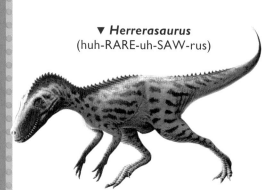

▲ *Plateosaurus*
(plate-e-o-SAW-rus)

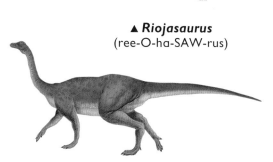

▲ *Riojasaurus*
(ree-O-ha-SAW-rus)

▲ *Melanorosaurus*
(me-lan-or-oh-SAW-rus)

▲ *Massospondylus*
(mass-oh-SPON-di-luss)

▼ Procompsognathus
(pro-comp-sog-NATH-us)

▲ Coelophysis
(see-low-FI-sis)

► Thecodontosaurus
(theek-o-don-toh-SAW-rus)

▲ Staurikosaurus
(stor-ik-oh-SAW-rus)

▲ Saltopus
(sal-to-pus)

▼ **Dilophosaurus**
(die-LOAF-o-SAW-rus)

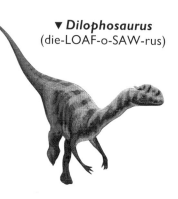

▼ **Barosaurus**
(bare-o-SAW-rus)

▼ **Rhoetosaurus**
(reet-oh-SAW-rus)

▼ *Eustreptospondylus*
(u-STREP-toe-spon-DI-lus)

▼ *Shunosaurus*
(shoo-no-SAW-rus)

▼ *Yunnanosaurus*
(yoo-nahn-oh-SAW-rus)

▶ *Anchisaurus*
(ANK-ee-saw-rus)

125

Jurassic dinosaurs 200–135 mya

▼ *Diplodocus*
(DI-plod-oh-kuss)

▼ *Kentrosaurus*
(ken-TROH-saw-rus)

◄ *Compsognathus*
(komp-sog-NATH-us)

► *Ceratosaurus*
(sir-RAT-oh-saw-rus)

▼ *Ornitholestes*
(or-ni-thoe-LESS-tees)

▼ Brachiosaurus
(brack-ee-o-SAW-rus)

▲ Tuojiangosaurus
(Two-oh-jee-ang-oh-SAW-rus)

◄ Apatosaurus
(ah-PAT-o-SAW-rus)

▼ Allosaurus
(AL-o-saw-rus)

▲ Coelurus
(seel-YEW-rus)

Cretaceous dinosaurs 120–65 mya

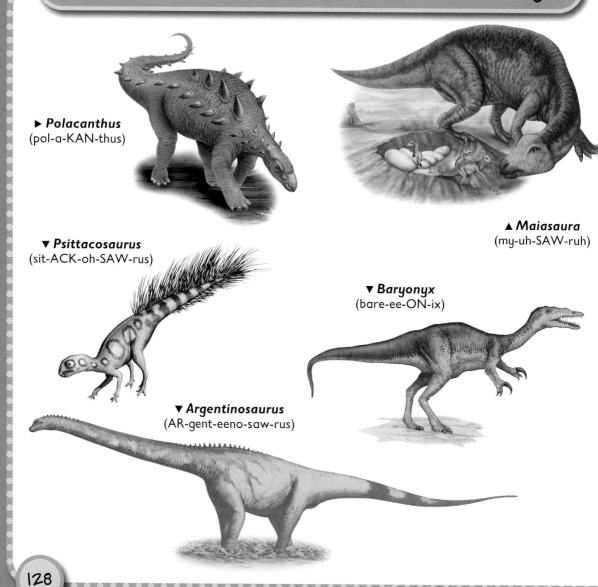

▶ **Polacanthus**
(pol-a-KAN-thus)

▲ **Maiasaura**
(my-uh-SAW-ruh)

▼ **Psittacosaurus**
(sit-ACK-oh-SAW-rus)

▼ **Baryonyx**
(bare-ee-ON-ix)

▼ **Argentinosaurus**
(AR-gent-eeno-saw-rus)

▼ Stegosaurus
(steg-o-SAW-rus)

▲ Spinosaurus
(spin-o-SAW-rus)

▲ Giganotosaurus
(jig-an-o-toe-SAW-rus)

▲ Caudipteryx
(caw-DIP-tuh-riks)

▲ Deinonychus
(die-NON-ee-kuss)

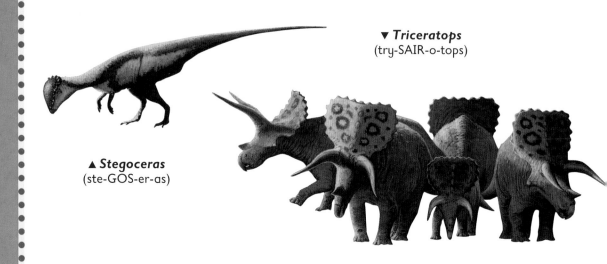

▼ Triceratops
(try-SAIR-o-tops)

▲ Stegoceras
(ste-GOS-er-as)

▶ Parasaurolophus
(pa-ra-saw-ROL-off-us)

▲ Protoceratops
(pro-toe-SAIR-o-tops)

▲ Ankylosaurus
(an-KIE-low-saw-rus)

▼ Saltasaurus
(salt-ah-SAW-rus)

◄ Lambeosaurus
(lam-bee-o-SAW-rus)

► Edmontonia
(ed-mon-TOE-nee-uh)

Cretaceous dinosaurs 120–65 mya

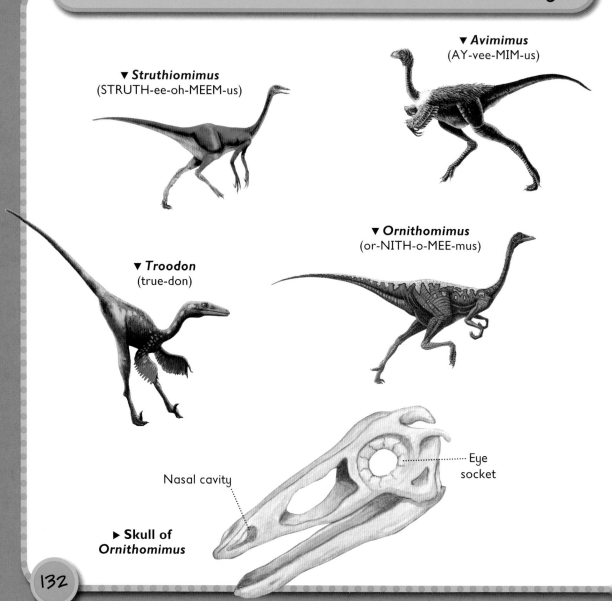

▼ *Avimimus*
(AY-vee-MIM-us)

▼ *Struthiomimus*
(STRUTH-ee-oh-MEEM-us)

▼ *Ornithomimus*
(or-NITH-o-MEE-mus)

▼ *Troodon*
(true-don)

Nasal cavity

Eye socket

▶ Skull of *Ornithomimus*

▼ Albertosaurus
(al-BERT-oh-saw-rus)

► Tyrannosaurus Rex
(tie-RAN-o-SAW-rus)

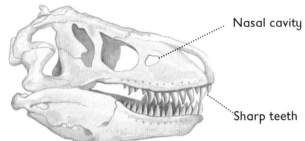

Nasal cavity

Sharp teeth

► Skull of
Tyrannosaurus Rex

Cretaceous eggs

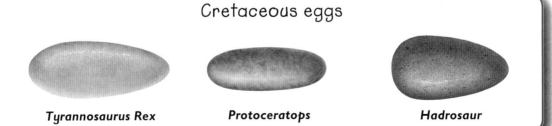

Tyrannosaurus Rex

Protoceratops

Hadrosaur

133

Prehistoric birds

▼ *Confuciusornis*

Long tail feathers

Sharp-toothed beak

Large head

▲ *Icthyornis*

▼ *Iberomesornis*

Long tail

Weak wing muscles

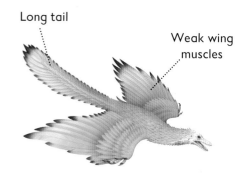

◄ *Waimanu*

▲ *Archaeopteryx*

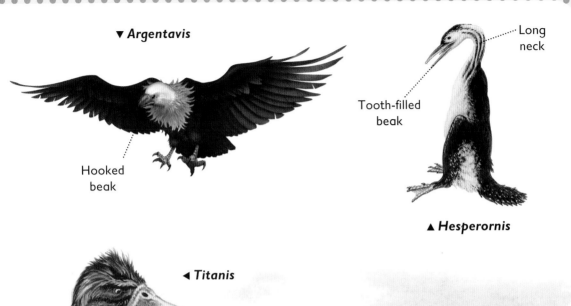

▼ *Argentavis*

Hooked beak

Long neck

Tooth-filled beak

▲ *Hesperornis*

◄ *Titanis*

◄ *Early horse*

135

Prehistoric mammals

▼ *Dinohyus*

▲ **Woolly rhinoceros**

▶ *Macrauchenia*

▶ *Megatherium*

◀ *Glyptodon*

▼ *Uintatherium*

▲ *Arsinoitherium*

▼ **Woolly mammoth**

▼ *Synthetoceras*

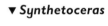

▲ *Hyracotherium*

Prehistoric mammals

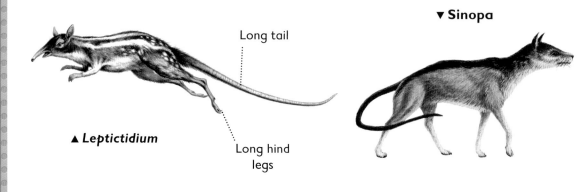

Long tail

▲ *Leptictidium*

Long hind legs

▼ **Sinopa**

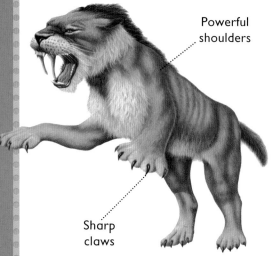

Powerful shoulders

Sharp claws

▲ *Smilodon*

▼ **Cave bear**

Bulky body

Strong jaws

▲ *Hesperocyon*

▼ *Andrewsarchus*

Strong
jaws

Clawed
feet

▼ *Potamotherium*

Bendy
backbone

Otter-like
body shape

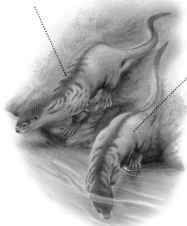

▲ *Megazostrodon*

Early primates

▼ *Plesiadapis*

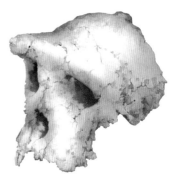

▲ **Skull of**
sahelanthropus tchadensis

▼ *Dryopithecus*

▼ *Ardipithecus ramidus*

▼ *Australopithecus afarensis*

▼ *Australopithecus africanus*

▼ *Paranthropus boisei*

▼ *Gigantopithecus*

The first humans

▼ *Homo habilis* skull

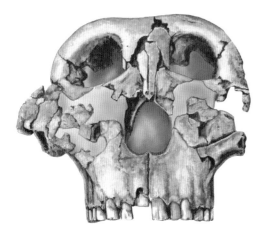

▶ *Homo ergaster*

▼ *Homo erectus*

▼ *Homo heidelbergensis*

▶ *Homo neanderthalensis*

Shorter, stockier bodies than modern humans

Used tools and weapons

Brain size comparison

Australopithecus afarensisthan

Homo habilis

Homo sapien

Plants

Plant kingdom

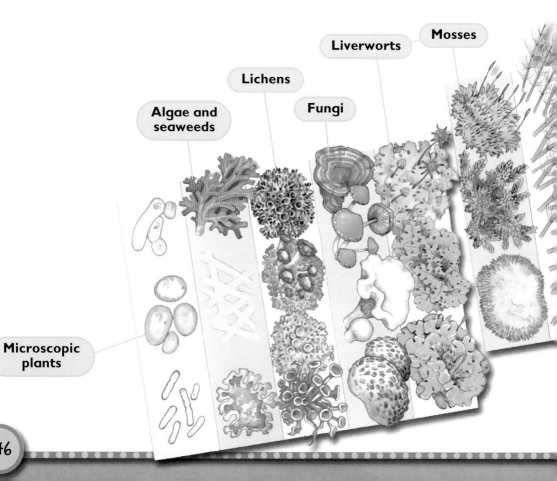

Mosses

Liverworts

Lichens

Fungi

Algae and
seaweeds

Microscopic
plants

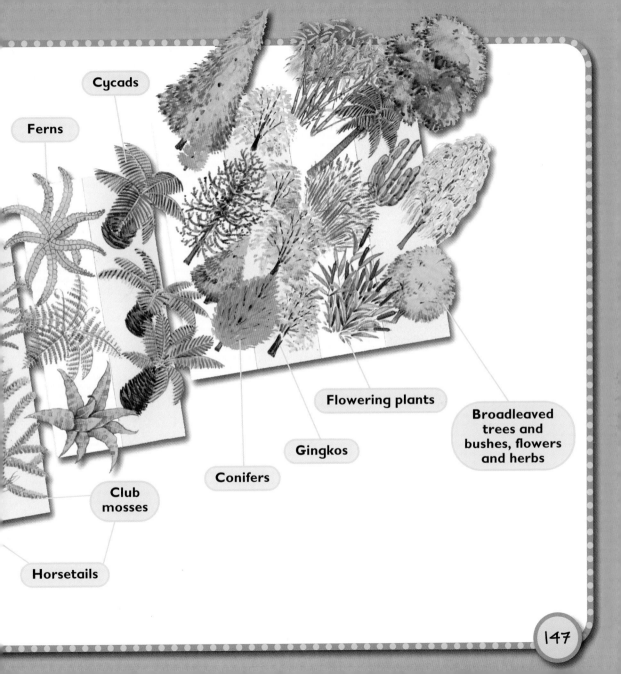

Cycads

Ferns

Flowering plants

Broadleaved
trees and
bushes, flowers
and herbs

Gingkos

Conifers

Club
mosses

Horsetails

Fungi

▼ Destroying angel
mushroom

▼ Chanterelle
mushroom

▼ Field
mushroom

▼ Fly agaric
toadstool

▼ Honey
mushroom

▼ Orange peel
fungus

▼ Earthstar
mushroom

▼ Puffball
fungus

▼ **Life cycle**

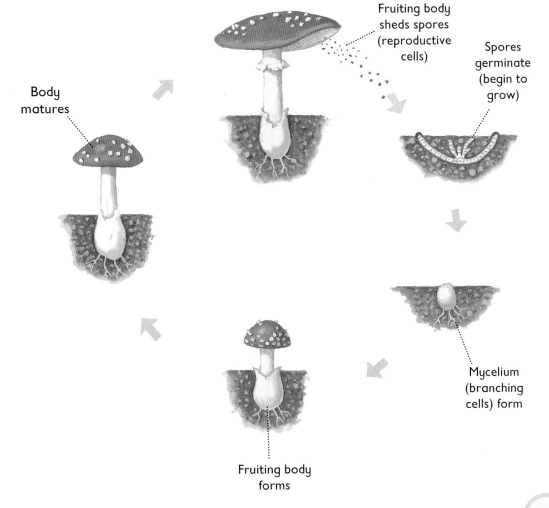

Body
matures

Fruiting body
sheds spores
(reproductive
cells)

Spores
germinate
(begin to
grow)

Mycelium
(branching
cells) form

Fruiting body
forms

Parts of a plant

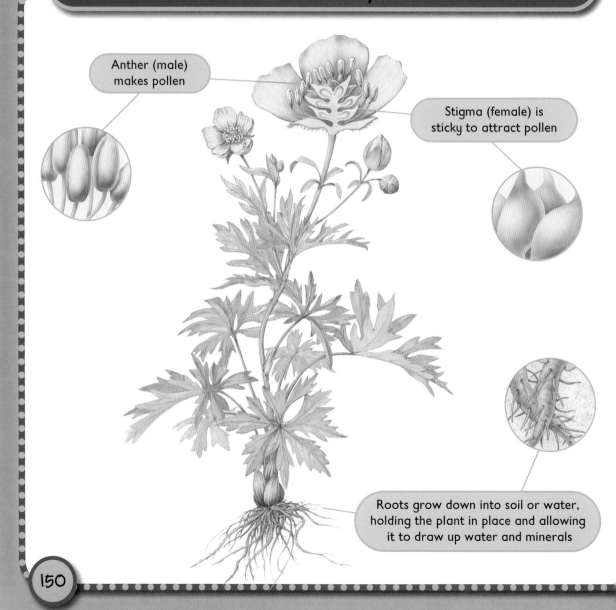

Anther (male) makes pollen

Stigma (female) is sticky to attract pollen

Roots grow down into soil or water, holding the plant in place and allowing it to draw up water and minerals

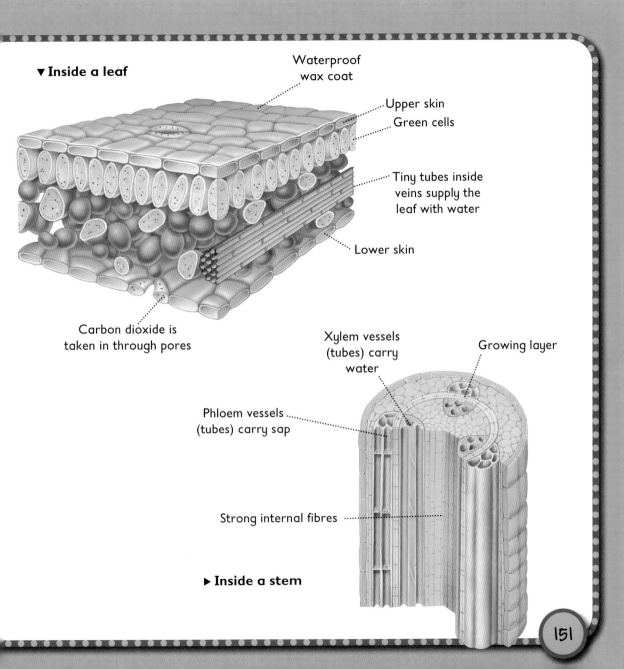

▼ Inside a leaf

Waterproof wax coat

Upper skin

Green cells

Tiny tubes inside veins supply the leaf with water

Lower skin

Carbon dioxide is taken in through pores

Xylem vessels (tubes) carry water

Growing layer

Phloem vessels (tubes) carry sap

Strong internal fibres

▶ Inside a stem

Photosynthesis

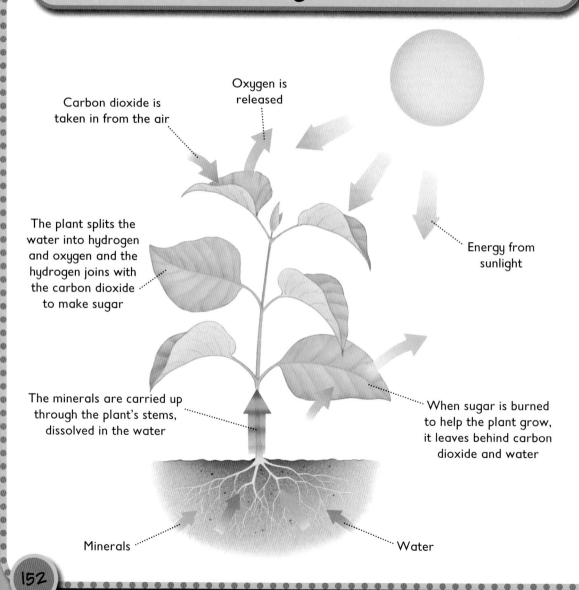

Carbon dioxide is taken in from the air

Oxygen is released

Energy from sunlight

The plant splits the water into hydrogen and oxygen and the hydrogen joins with the carbon dioxide to make sugar

When sugar is burned to help the plant grow, it leaves behind carbon dioxide and water

The minerals are carried up through the plant's stems, dissolved in the water

Minerals

Water

Leaves

▼ **Walnut tree**

▼ **Horse chestnut tree**

▼ **Willow tree**

▼ **Apple tree**

▼ **English oak tree**

Plant reproduction

▼ **Germination**

I. The seed lies dormant until conditions are right

Shoot ....

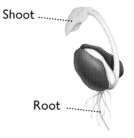

Root ....

2. The seed sends a root down and a shoot up

Cotyledon

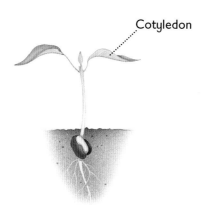

3. The shoot bursts into the air and grows cotyledons (seed leaves)

4. The stem and roots grow longer, and the plant soon begins to grow new leaves

▼ Parts of a flower

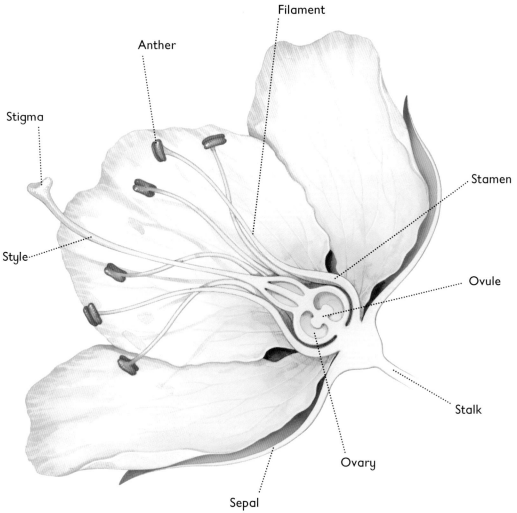

Filament

Anther

Stigma

Stamen

Style

Ovule

Stalk

Ovary

Sepal

Plant life cycles

▼ Mosses

1. Male sperm cells join the female egg

2. One sperm cell unites with the female egg cell

3. The fertilized egg grows into a stalk (sporophyte) with a capsule on top, which holds thousands of spores

4. The sporophyte capsule bursts

5. The process begins again

▼ Annual plant

1. Seed capsule

2. The seedling germinates

3. Buds form

4. Plant flowers and seeds form

▼ Biennial plant

1. The plant grows for one year

2. Buds form

3. Flowers begin to open

4. Flower blooms

5. Flowers pollinate and are fertilized

6. Seeds form and are dispersed

7. Seeds grow in the ground

8. The seedling germinates

Carnivorous plants

▼ Sundew

Digestive juices dissolve insects that land on the sticky tentacles

Jawlike leaves

Nectar lures the insect in

Once the insect lands, the 'jaws' clamp shut on the victim

▶ Venus fly-trap

Plant defences

▼ Pebble plants
Thick round leaves that look like pebbles provide camouflage

▲ Water hemlock
Poisonous

▼ Nettle
Stinging hairs provide protection from animals

► Prickly pear
Sharp spines prevent animals from reaching the water stored in the stems

Primitive plants

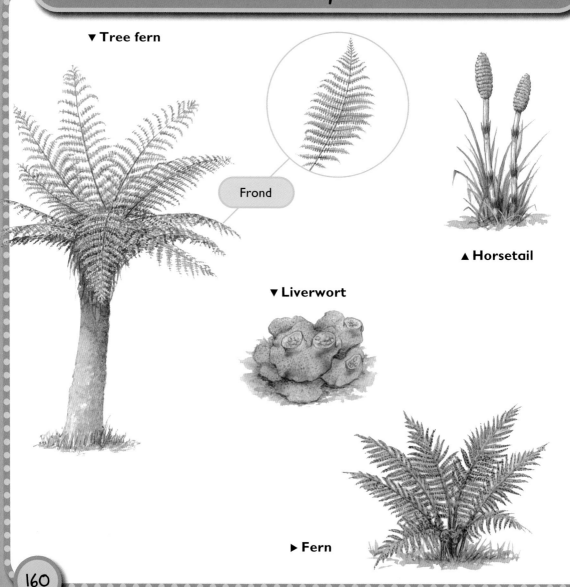

▼ Tree fern

Frond

▲ Horsetail

▼ Liverwort

► Fern

Grasses

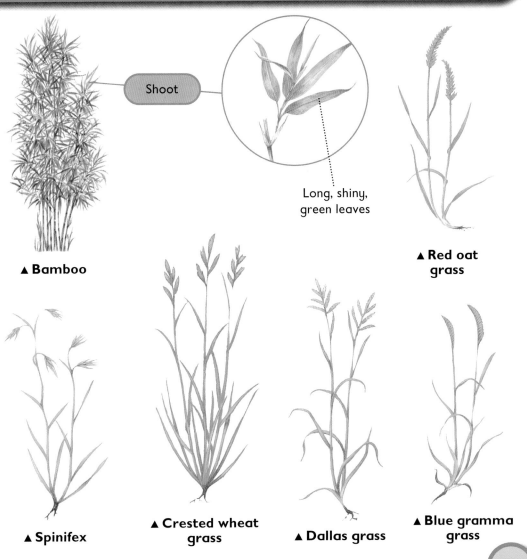

Shoot

Long, shiny, green leaves

▲ Bamboo

▲ Red oat grass

▲ Spinifex

▲ Crested wheat grass

▲ Dallas grass

▲ Blue gramma grass

Evergreen trees

▲ Corsican pine

Narrow, cone-shaped crown

▲ Holly

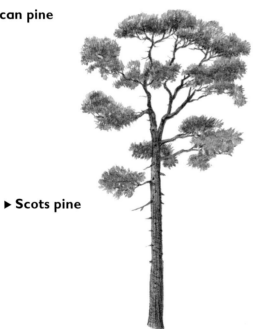

▶ Scots pine

▲ Coast redwood

▲ Eucalyptus

▶ Douglas fir

▼ Larch

▲ Mountain ash

Herbs

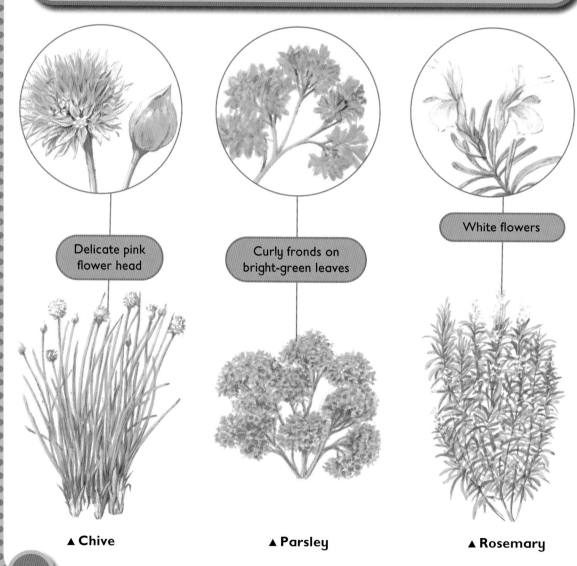

Delicate pink flower head

Curly fronds on bright-green leaves

White flowers

▲ Chive

▲ Parsley

▲ Rosemary

▼ **Herbs used in cooking**

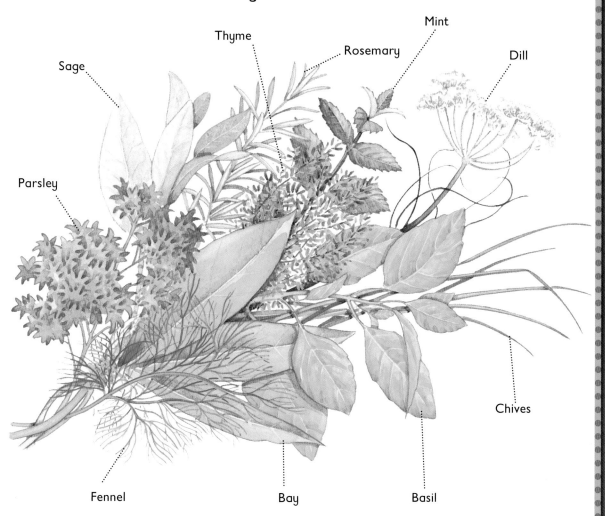

Sage

Thyme

Rosemary

Mint

Dill

Parsley

Fennel

Bay

Basil

Chives

Shrubs

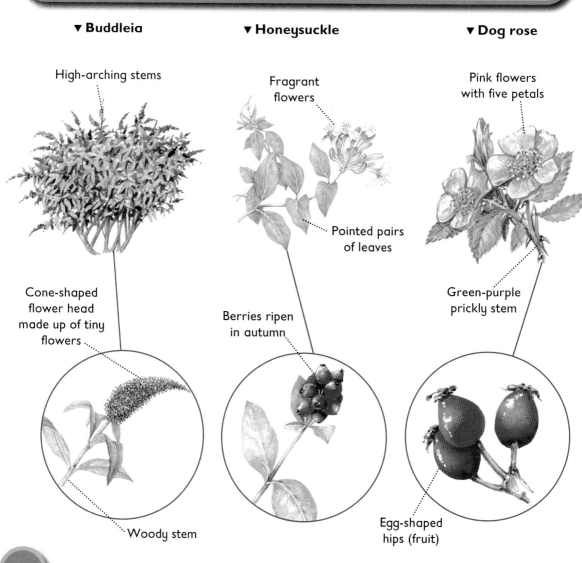

▼ Buddleia

High-arching stems

Cone-shaped flower head made up of tiny flowers

Woody stem

▼ Honeysuckle

Fragrant flowers

Pointed pairs of leaves

Berries ripen in autumn

▼ Dog rose

Pink flowers with five petals

Green-purple prickly stem

Egg-shaped hips (fruit)

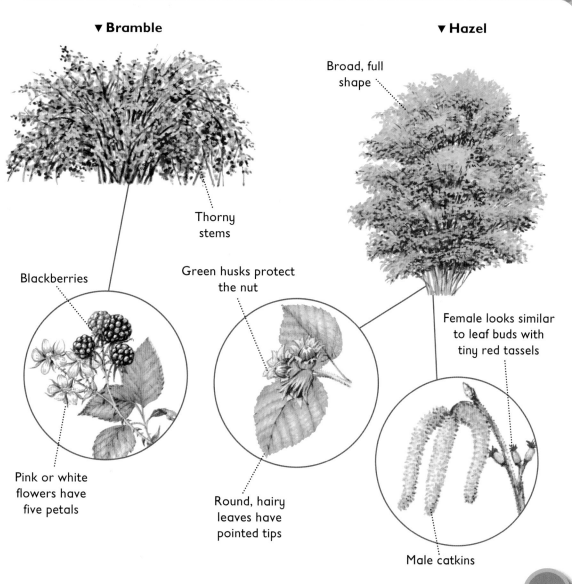

▼ Bramble

Thorny stems

Blackberries

Pink or white flowers have five petals

Green husks protect the nut

Round, hairy leaves have pointed tips

▼ Hazel

Broad, full shape

Female looks similar to leaf buds with tiny red tassels

Male catkins

167

Flowers

Flower opening

1. The flower is packed away inside a bud. Green flaps (sepals) wrap tightly around it.

2. The bud begins to open. The sepals curl back to reveal colourful petals.

3. The sepals open wide and the petals grow out.

4. The flower opens fully, revealing its pollen sacs (anthers).

▼ **Garlic mustard**

▶ **Clematis**

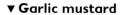

Small, snow-white flowers

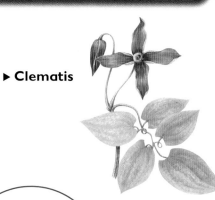

▼ **Bluebell**

Flowers hang, or droop, from stems

▶ **Foxglove**

▶ **Lesser celandine**

▼ **Dandelion**

▼ **Bindweed**

Flowers

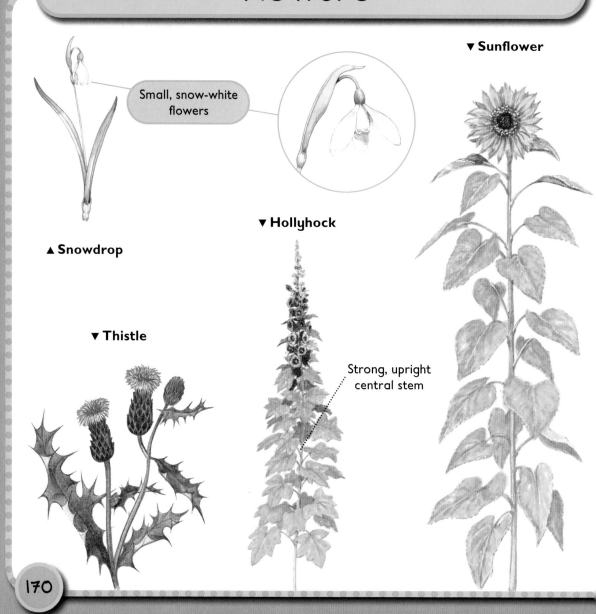

Small, snow-white flowers

▼ Sunflower

▼ Hollyhock

▲ Snowdrop

▼ Thistle

Strong, upright central stem

▼ Primrose

Flowers grow from the base of the plant on long stalks

▼ Hosta

▼ Poppy

Holes open in the heads, allowing seeds to fall through

▼ Wood anemone

Deciduous trees

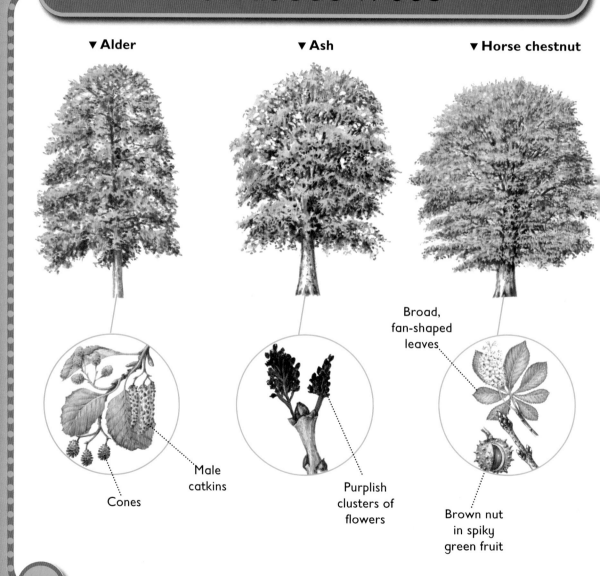

▼ Alder

▼ Ash

▼ Horse chestnut

Broad, fan-shaped leaves

Male catkins

Cones

Purplish clusters of flowers

Brown nut in spiky green fruit

▼ Pendunculate oak

▼ Rowan

Female flowers

Male catkins

Acorns sit in
cups at the end
of long stalks

Small, white
flowers in
dense clusters

Animals

Molluscs and bivalves

▼ Garden snail

Hard shell protects against predators

Two pairs of sensitive tentacles

▲ Burrowing slug

▼ Giant African snail

▼ Cone shell

Mouth tube shoots a poisonous dart into prey

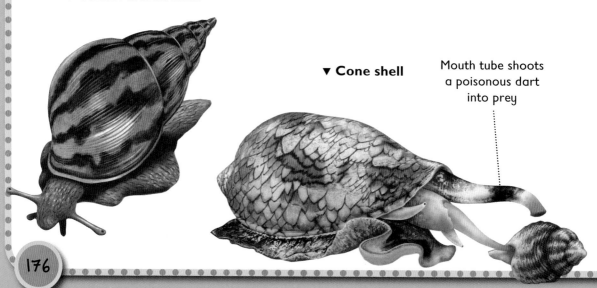

Cephalopods

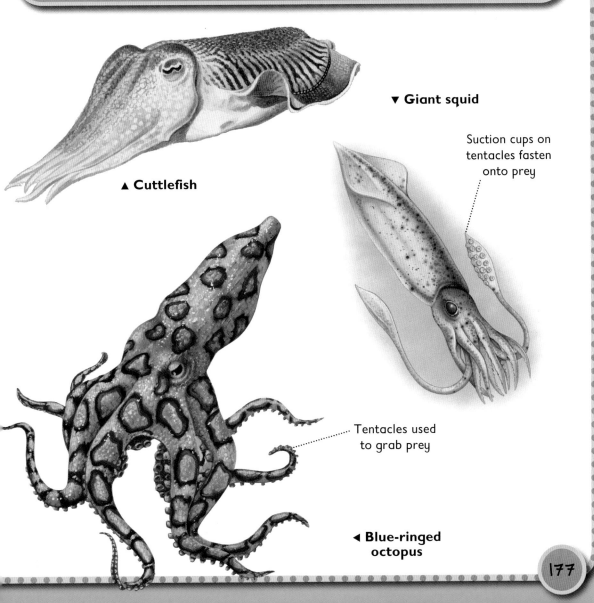

▲ Cuttlefish

▼ Giant squid

Suction cups on tentacles fasten onto prey

Tentacles used to grab prey

◄ Blue-ringed octopus

177

Spider anatomy

▼ **Funnelweb spider**

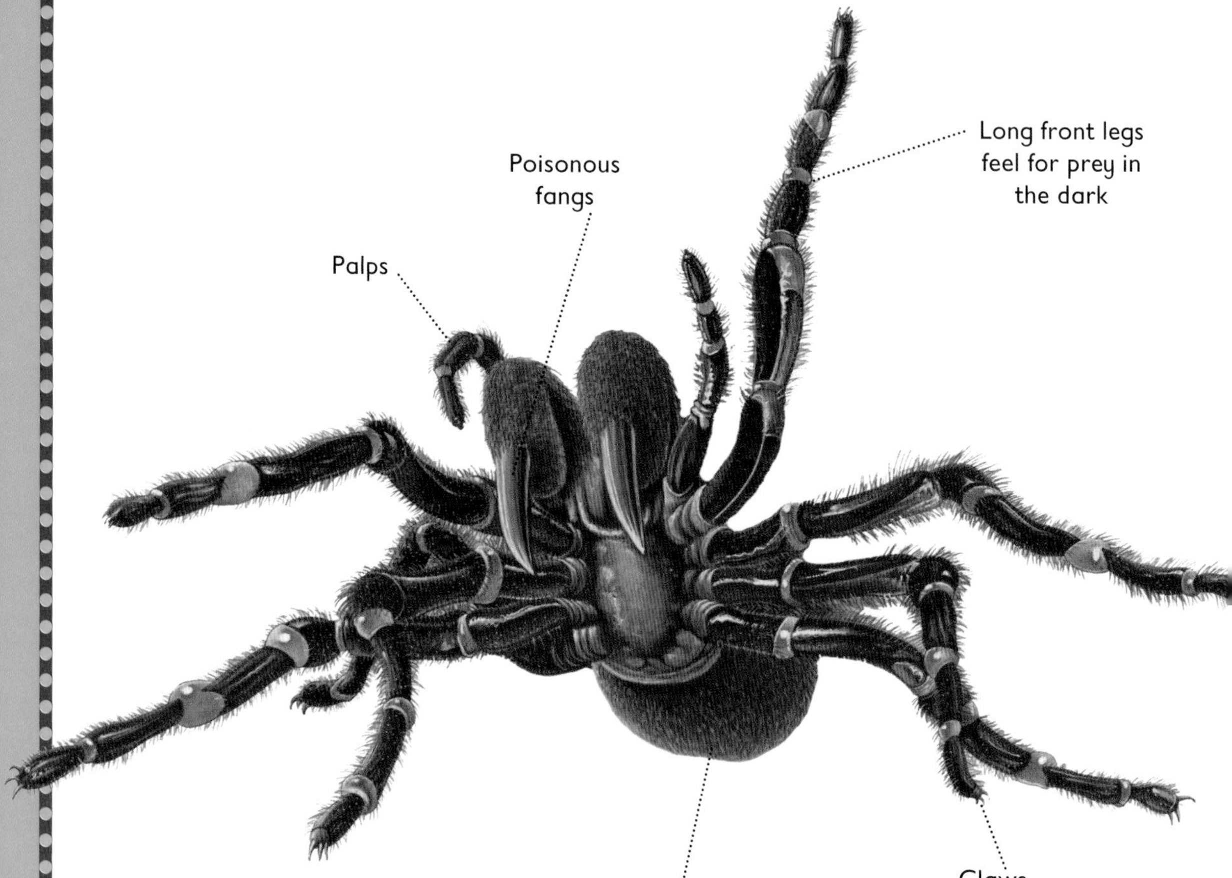

Long front legs feel for prey in the dark
Poisonous fangs
Palps
Abdomen
Claws

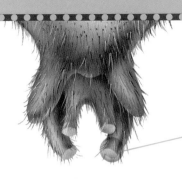

 Spinneret

Spigots produce
coarse silk for
making webs

Spools produce fine
silk for wrapping prey

▼ **Making a web**

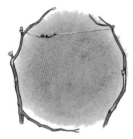

1. A spider starts a web
by building a bridge

2. Then it makes a
triangle shape

3. It adds more threads to
make a strong framework

4. Finally, the spider fills the
frame with circular threads

5. The finished web is strong
enough to catch large insects

Spider behaviour

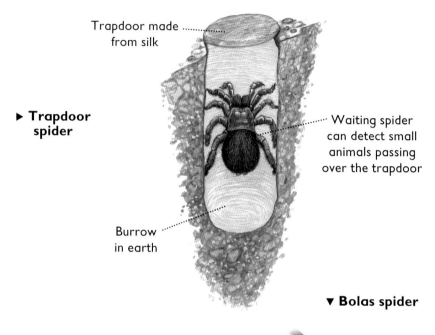

Trapdoor made from silk

▶ **Trapdoor spider**

Waiting spider can detect small animals passing over the trapdoor

Burrow in earth

▼ **Bolas spider**

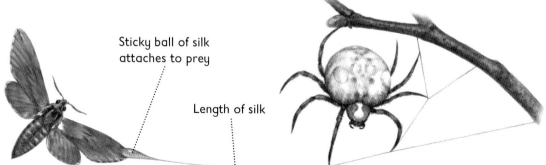

Sticky ball of silk attaches to prey

Length of silk

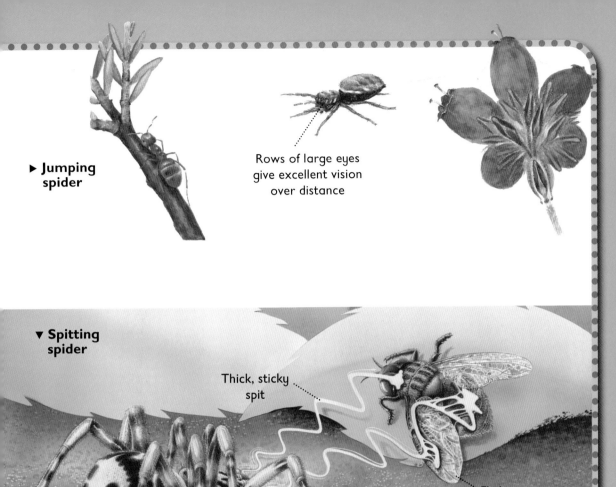

▶ **Jumping spider**

Rows of large eyes give excellent vision over distance

▼ **Spitting spider**

Thick, sticky spit

Fly becomes entangled

Spiders

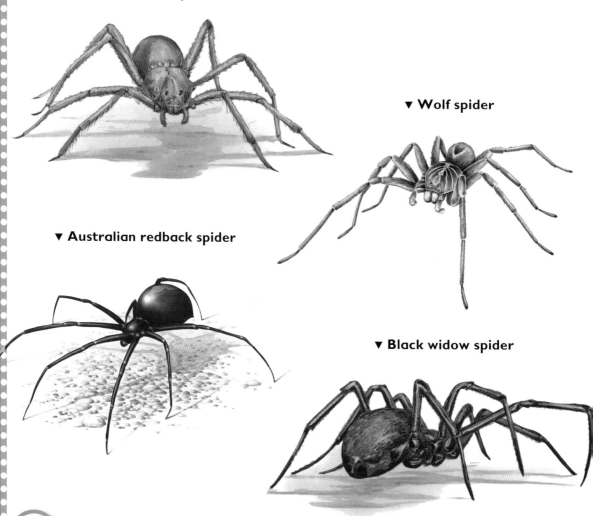

▼ Violin spider

▼ Wolf spider

▼ Australian redback spider

▼ Black widow spider

▲ Tarantula

▶ Orb-web spider

▲ Flower spider

Spiders

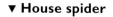

▲ **Raft spider**

▼ **House spider**

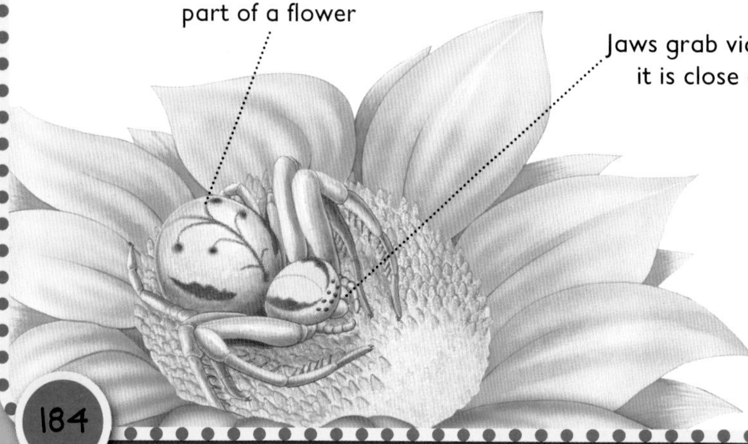

Wide body, coloured
and shaped to look like
part of a flower

Jaws grab victim when
it is close enough

◄ **Crab spider**

184

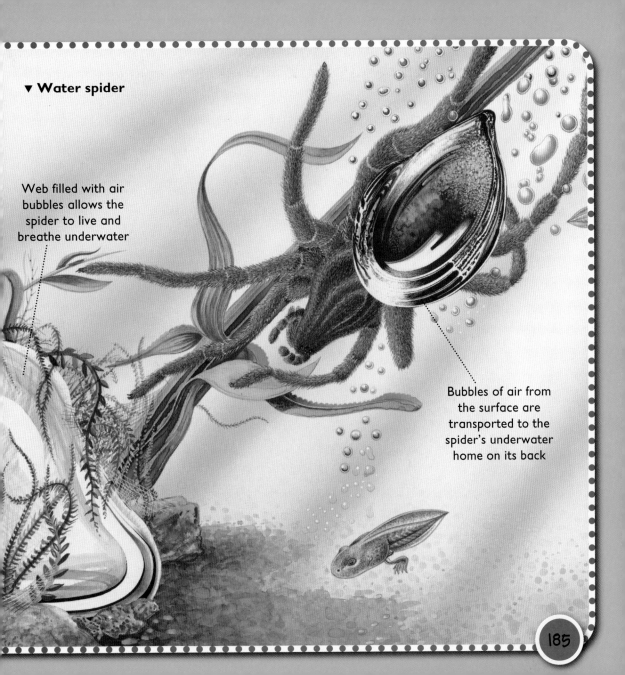

▼ **Water spider**

Web filled with air
bubbles allows the
spider to live and
breathe underwater

Bubbles of air from
the surface are
transported to the
spider's underwater
home on its back

185

▼ **Death stalker scorpion**

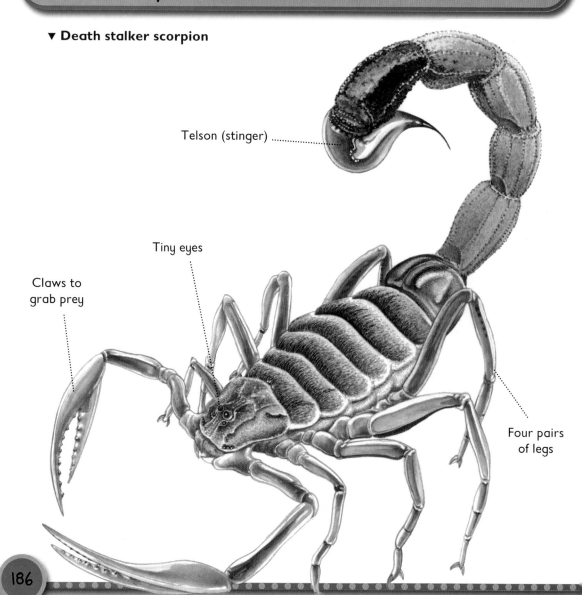

Telson (stinger)

Tiny eyes

Claws to grab prey

Four pairs of legs

186

▼ Harvestman

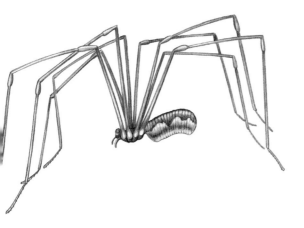

Flat
body

▲ Tick

▼ False scorpion

Poisonous
pincers

▲ Velvet mite

Crustaceans

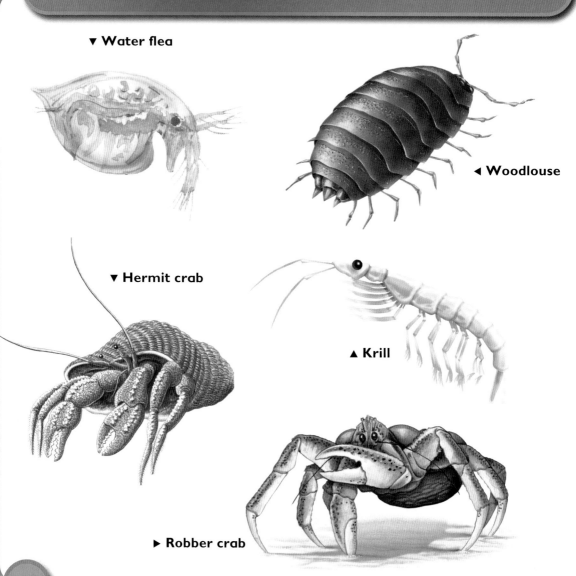

▼ Water flea

◀ Woodlouse

▼ Hermit crab

▲ Krill

▶ Robber crab

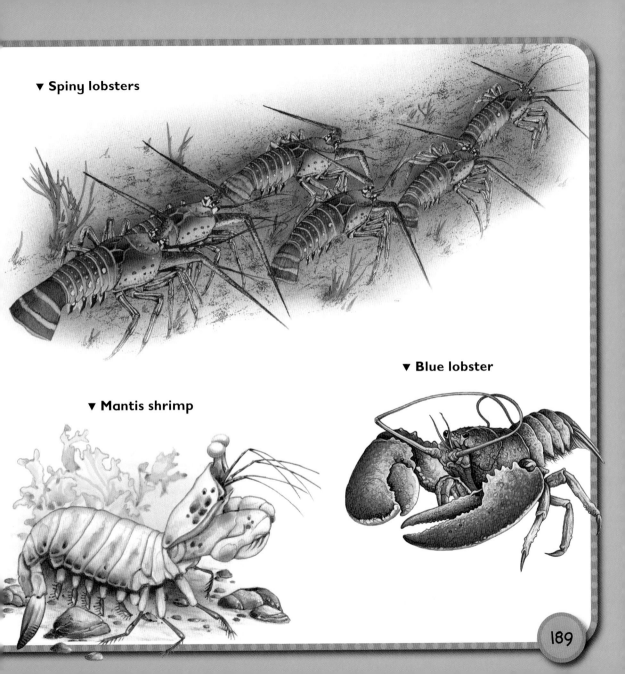

▼ Spiny lobsters

▼ Blue lobster

▼ Mantis shrimp

189

Flies and dragonflies

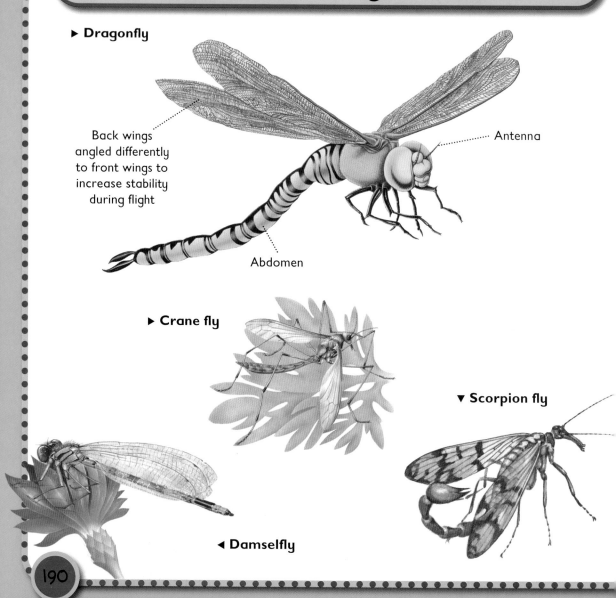

▶ **Dragonfly**

Back wings
angled differently
to front wings to
increase stability
during flight

Antenna

Abdomen

▶ **Crane fly**

▼ **Scorpion fly**

◀ **Damselfly**

▶ Mosquito

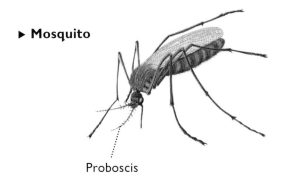

Proboscis

▼ Horse fly

▲ Lantern fly

▼ Bee fly

▼ House fly

Bloodsucker

Tsetse flies feed on blood and spread parasites that cause sleeping sickness.

Before bloodsucking

After bloodsucking

Crickets and grasshoppers

▼ **Inside a grasshopper**

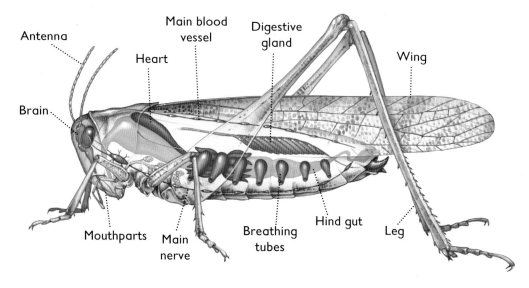

Antenna

Heart

Main blood vessel

Digestive gland

Wing

Brain

Mouthparts

Main nerve

Breathing tubes

Hind gut

Leg

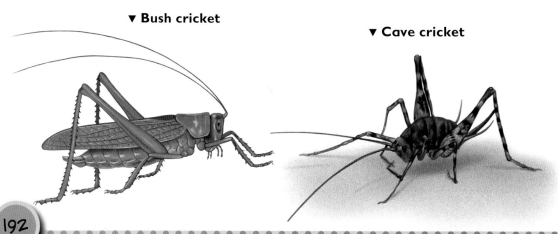

▼ **Bush cricket**

▼ **Cave cricket**

Mantises and cockroaches

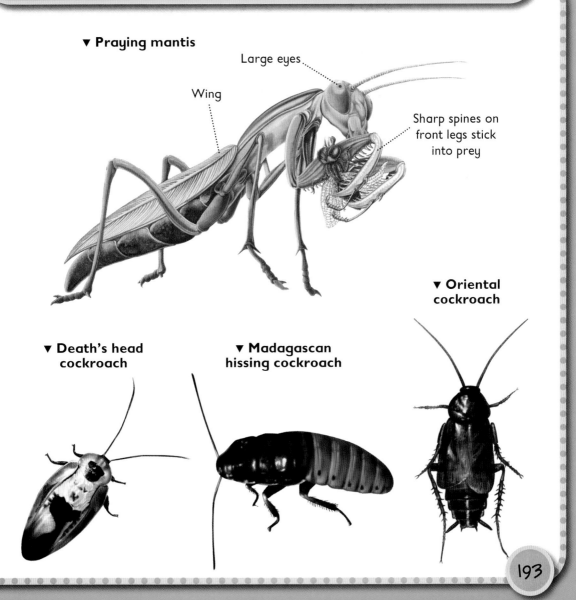

▼ **Praying mantis**

Large eyes

Wing

Sharp spines on front legs stick into prey

▼ **Oriental cockroach**

▼ **Death's head cockroach**

▼ **Madagascan hissing cockroach**

Termites and earwigs

▼ **Common earwig**

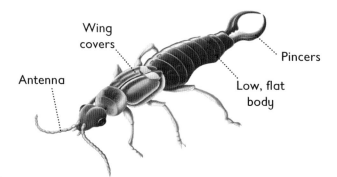

Wing covers

Antenna

Pincers

Low, flat body

Earwig behaviour

Natural tail position

When the earwig feels threatened, it raises its tail

◀ **Termite mound**

▶ **Wood termite**

Beetles

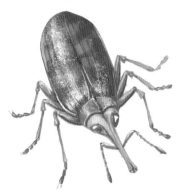

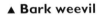

▲ **Bark weevil**

▼ **Scarab beetle**

▲ **Goliath beetle**

▶ **Bombardier beetle**

When threatened,
Bombardier beetles twist the
ends of their abdomens to
squirt a boiling, irritating
liquid in almost any direction.

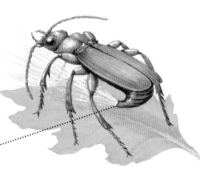

195

Beetles

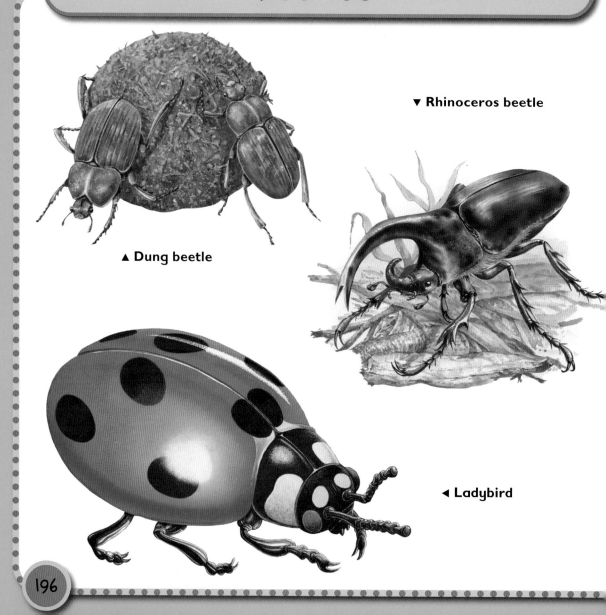

▼ Rhinoceros beetle

▲ Dung beetle

◄ Ladybird

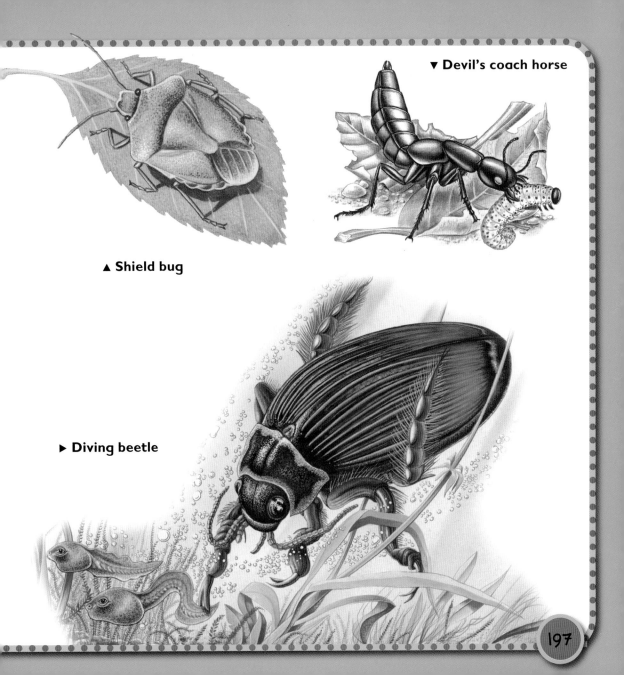

▼ **Devil's coach horse**

▲ **Shield bug**

▶ **Diving beetle**

197

Butterfly life cycle

1. Egg laid by a fertilized adult female butterfly

2. The egg hatches into a tiny larva (caterpillar)

3. The caterpillar attaches itself to a twig and forms a hard outer shell (chrysalis)

5. Adults have a short lifespan. They will fly, mate and reproduce before they die

4. Inside the chrysalis, the caterpillar changes into a butterfly, and emerges as a fully grown adult

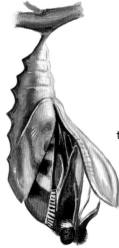

Caterpillars

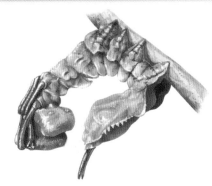

▲ **Lobster moth caterpillar**

▼ **Geometrid moth caterpillar**

◄ **Death's head hawk moth caterpillar**

▼ **Large white caterpillar**

▲ **Isabella tiger moth caterpillar**

Butterflies

▲ Camberwell beauty butterfly

▶ Orange tip butterfly

◀ Peacock butterfly

▼ Apollo butterfly

▶ Holly blue butterfly

◄ Red admiral
butterfly

▼ Brimstone
butterfly

► Comma
butterfly

► Rajah Brook's
Birdwing butterfly

Butterflies

◄ Small
tortoiseshell
butterfly

▼ Monarch butterfly

▼ Speckled wood
butterfly

◄ Bhutan glory
butterfly

▶ Painted
lady butterfly

Moths

▼ **Death's head hawk moth**

▲ **White peppered moth**

▼ **Moon moth**

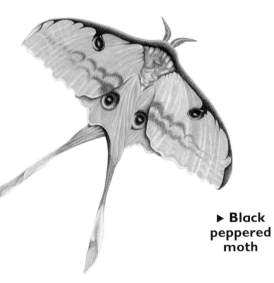

▶ **Darwin's hawk moth**

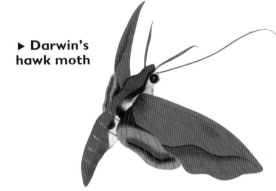

▶ **Black peppered moth**

Ants

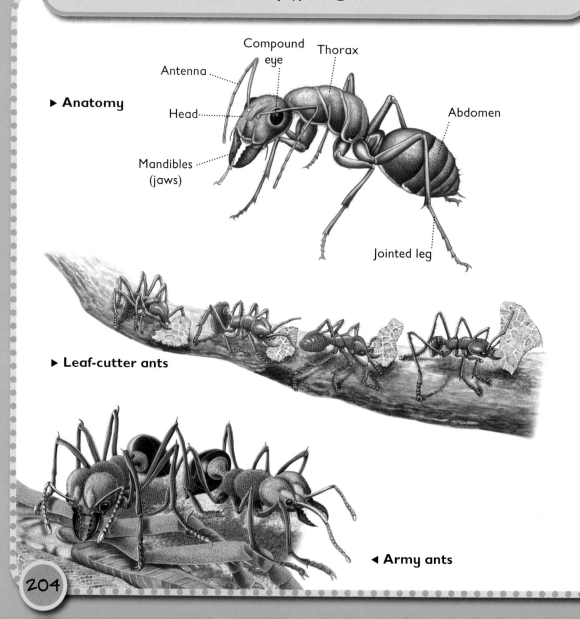

▶ **Anatomy**

Antenna

Compound eye

Thorax

Head

Abdomen

Mandibles (jaws)

Jointed leg

▶ **Leaf-cutter ants**

◀ **Army ants**

Bees

▼ Anatomy

Antenna
Head
Compound eye
Wing
Thorax
Leg
Abdomen

▲ Mason bee

◄ Leafcutter bee

▼ Carpenter bee

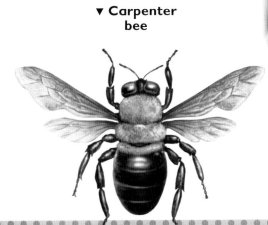

► Honey bee

Wasps

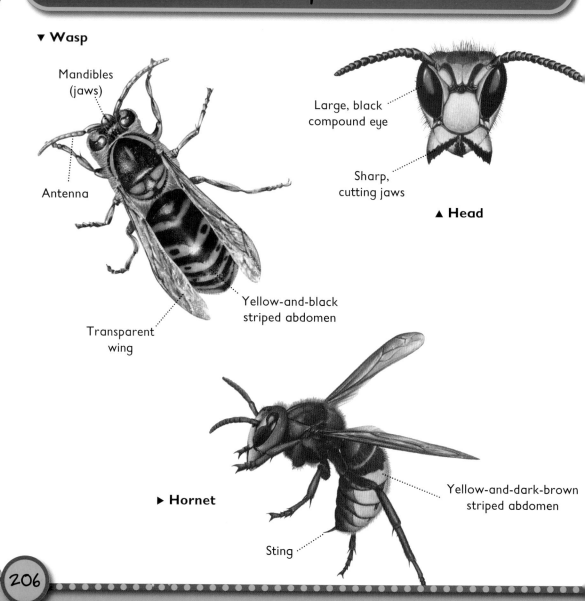

▼ **Wasp**

Mandibles (jaws)

Antenna

Transparent wing

Yellow-and-black striped abdomen

Large, black compound eye

Sharp, cutting jaws

▲ **Head**

▶ **Hornet**

Yellow-and-dark-brown striped abdomen

Sting

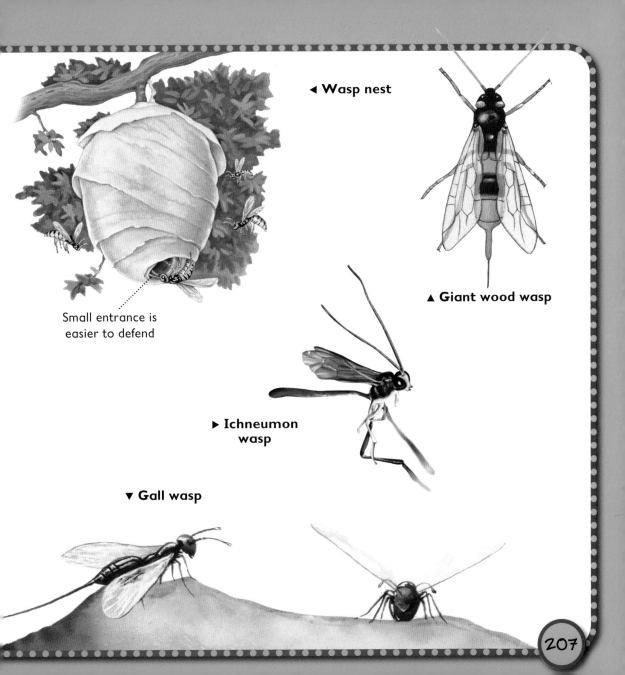

◄ **Wasp nest**

Small entrance is
easier to defend

▲ **Giant wood wasp**

▶ **Ichneumon
wasp**

▼ **Gall wasp**

207

Shark anatomy

▼ **Main organs and body parts**

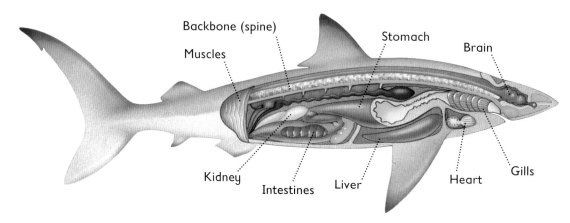

Backbone (spine)

Muscles

Stomach

Brain

Kidney

Intestines

Liver

Heart

Gills

▼ **Skeleton**

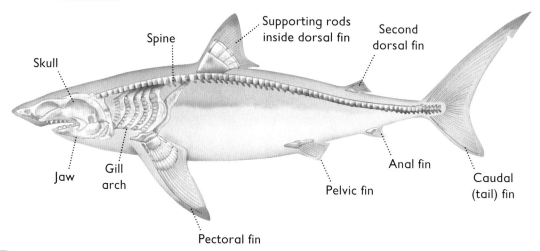

Supporting rods inside dorsal fin

Second dorsal fin

Spine

Skull

Jaw

Gill arch

Anal fin

Caudal (tail) fin

Pelvic fin

Pectoral fin

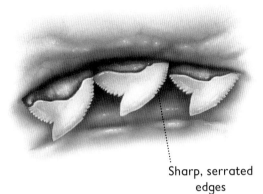

▼ **Teeth**

Sharp, serrated
edges

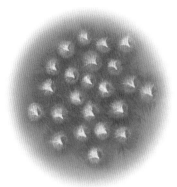

▲ **Magnified view of denticles**
Tiny hard points called 'denticles' cover
a shark's skin. They protect the skin and
help the shark to slide through the water.

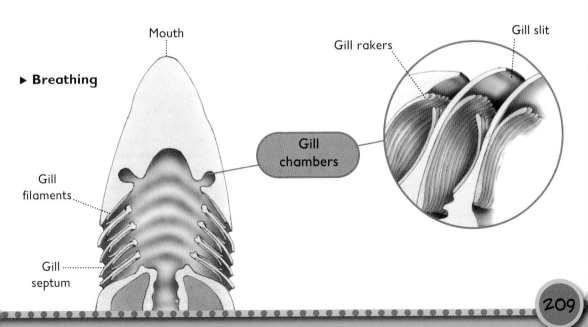

Mouth

Gill rakers

Gill slit

► **Breathing**

Gill
chambers

Gill
filaments

Gill
septum

Shark development

50 days

100 days

150 days

200 days

Store
of food
(yolk)

500 days

▲ **Development of Catshark young**
Some sharks, such as the Catshark,
lay eggs, while others give birth to live
young known as 'pups'.

Sharks

▼ **Porbeagle shark**

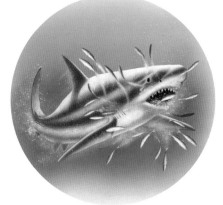

▲ **Bull shark**

▶ **Zebra shark**

▼ **Cookie-cutter shark head**

Circular
mouth

▼ **Cookie-cutter shark**

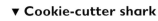

Sharks

▼ Crocodile shark

▲ Black-tip shark

▼ Bramble shark

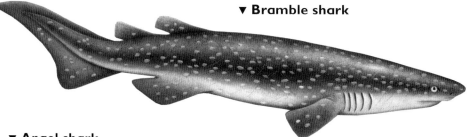

▼ Angel shark

▲ Dogfish shark

◄ Sand tiger shark

► Goblin shark

▼ Epaulette shark

◄ Great white shark

▼ Horn shark

213

Sharks

▼ Greenland shark

▶ Bonnethead shark

▼ Spiny pygmy shark
These sharks work in groups to attack sick or injured fish much larger than themselves.

▼ Lemon shark

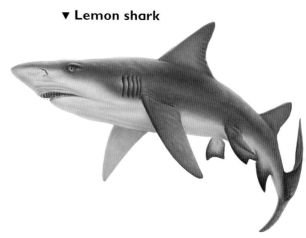

▼ Blind shark

▲ Frilled shark

▶ Blue shark

▼ Mako shark

▲ Weasel shark

215

Skates and rays

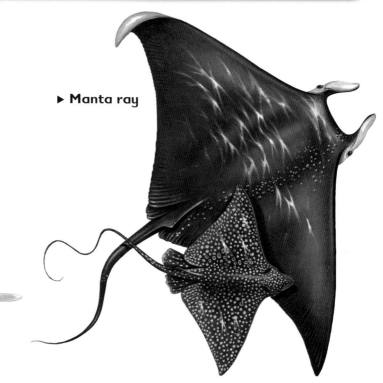

▲ Common skate

▶ Manta ray

▲ Spotted eagle ray

▶ Sawfish

Fish anatomy

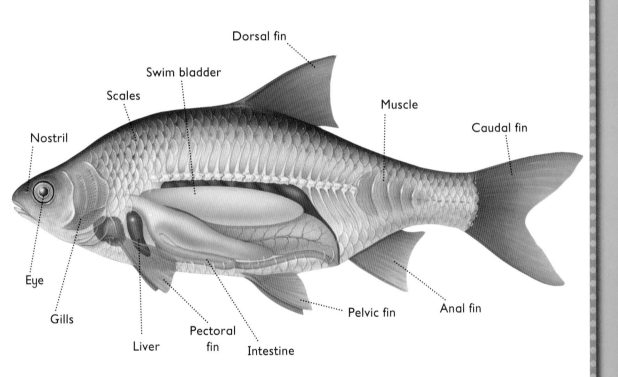

Dorsal fin

Swim bladder

Scales

Muscle

Caudal fin

Nostril

Eye

Gills

Liver

Pectoral fin

Intestine

Pelvic fin

Anal fin

Fish

▼ Cod

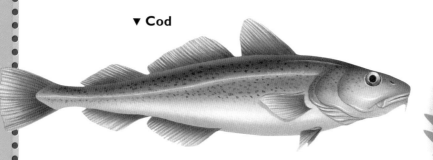

▼ Spiny puffer fish
When threatened, the spiny puffer fish
swallows large amounts of water, making
its body swell up and its spines stand on end.

▲ Herring

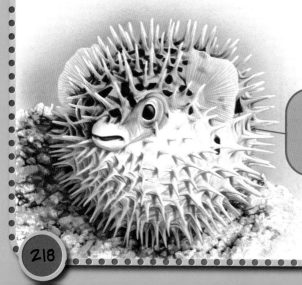

When the danger
has passed, the fish
exhales the water
and returns to
normal size

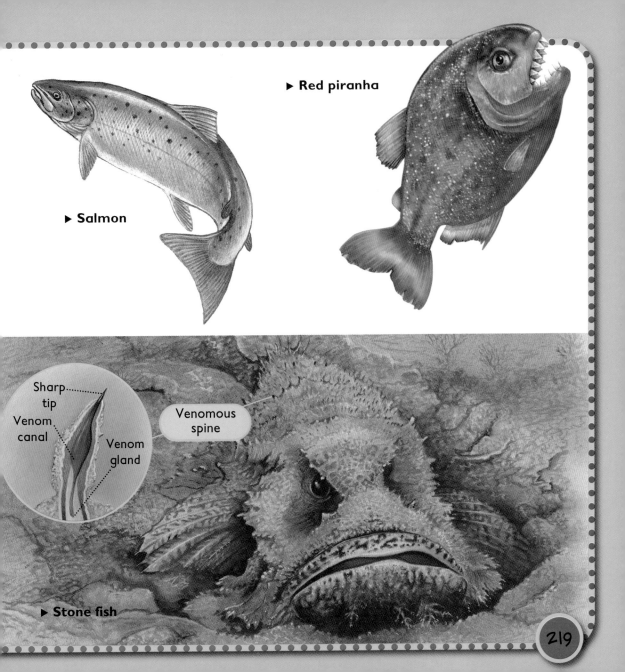

▶ Red piranha

▶ Salmon

Sharp tip

Venom canal

Venom gland

Venomous spine

▶ Stone fish

219

Fish

▼ Black swallower

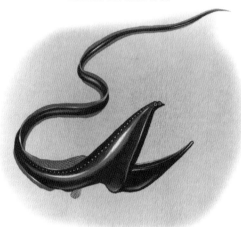

▲ Sun fish

▼ Yellow snapper

◄ Oarfish

◄ Lanternfish

► Dragon fish

▼ Angler fish

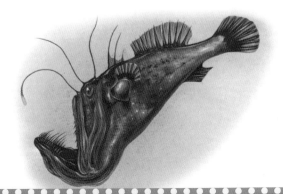

▼ Viperfish

221

Fish

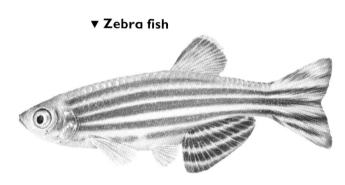
▼ Zebra fish

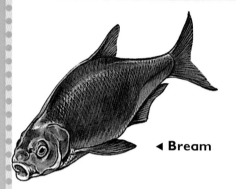
◀ Bream

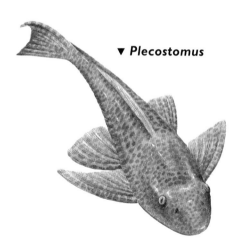
▼ Plecostomus

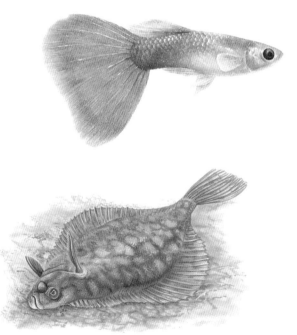
▼ Guppy

▶ Flatfish

222

▼ Red-tailed shark

▲ Koi carp

▲ Flying fish

▼ Sturgeon

223

Frogs

▲ Strawberry
poison dart frog

▲ Green poison
dart frog

▲ Malaysian
horned frog

▲ Natal ghost frog

▲ Tree frog

▲ American
bullfrog

224

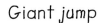
Giant jump

1. The powerful muscles in the frog's hind legs push off

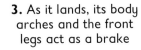

3. As it lands, its body arches and the front legs act as a brake

2. In mid-leap, the hind legs are fully stretched out and the front legs are held back

▲ **Golden arrow-poison frog**

▲ **Goliath frog**

▲ **Arum lily frog**

Toads

▼ Natterjack toad

▲ Marine toad

▼ Giant toad

▲ Common toad

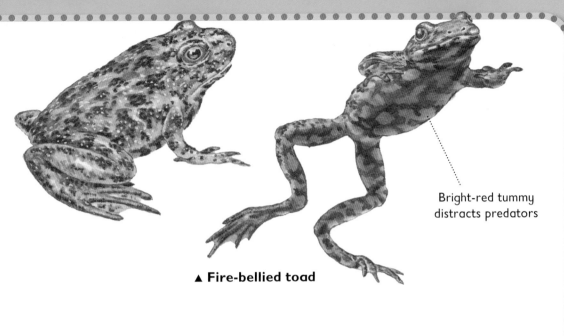

Bright-red tummy
distracts predators

▲ Fire-bellied toad

► Cane toad

Amphibian reproduction

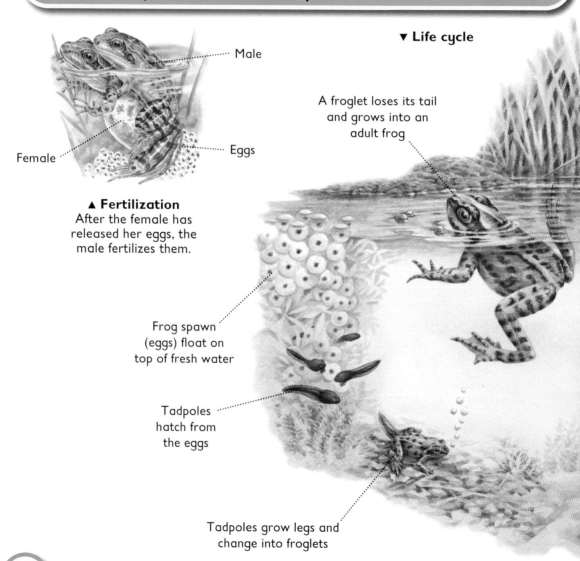

Male

Female

Eggs

▲ **Fertilization**
After the female has released her eggs, the male fertilizes them.

▼ **Life cycle**

A froglet loses its tail and grows into an adult frog

Frog spawn (eggs) float on top of fresh water

Tadpoles hatch from the eggs

Tadpoles grow legs and change into froglets

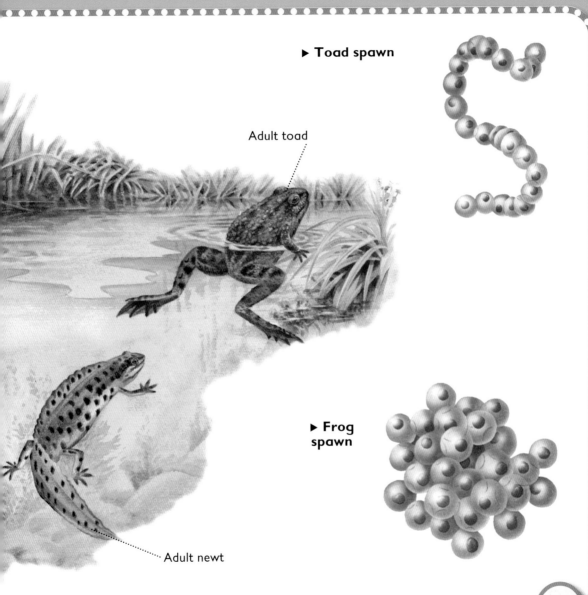

▶ **Toad spawn**

Adult toad

Adult newt

▶ **Frog spawn**

Salamanders and newts

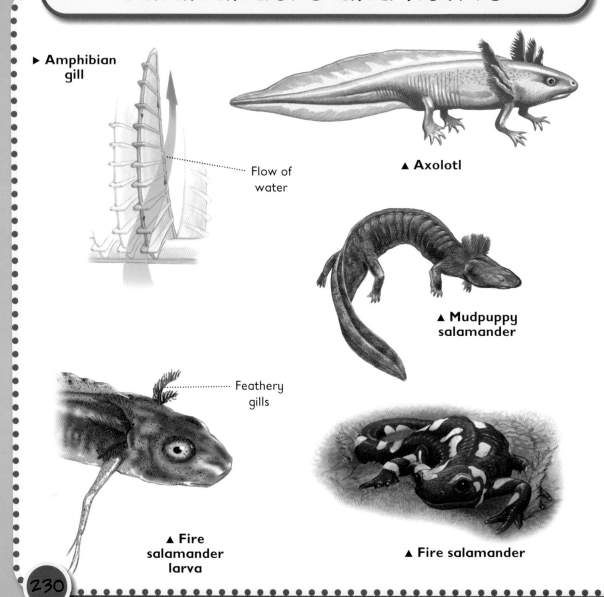

► Amphibian gill

Flow of water

▲ Axolotl

▲ Mudpuppy salamander

Feathery gills

▲ Fire salamander larva

▲ Fire salamander

▲ Hellbender

▼ Californian newt

▲ Rough-skinned newt

▼ Eastern newt

▲ Great crested newt

231

Crocodiles

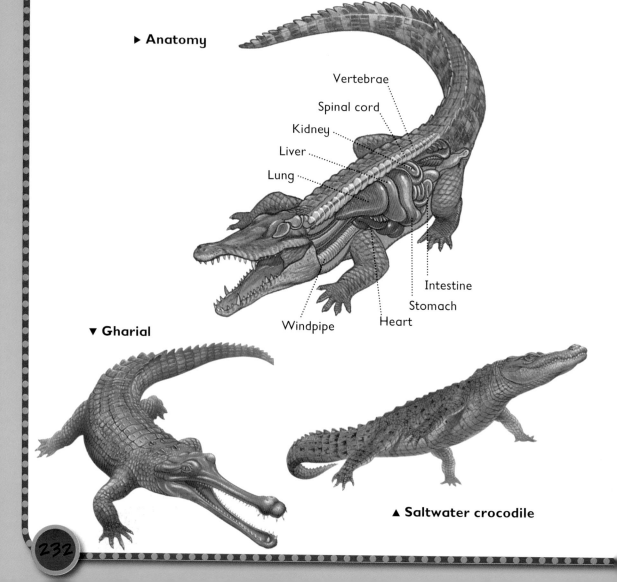

▶ **Anatomy**

Vertebrae

Spinal cord

Kidney

Liver

Lung

Windpipe

Heart

Stomach

Intestine

▼ **Gharial**

▲ **Saltwater crocodile**

▼ Mugger

▼ West African
dwarf crocodile

▼ Nile crocodile

233

Alligators

◀ **Common caiman**

▶ **Spectacled caiman**

Spot the difference

Teeth in the lower jaw can be seen

Only teeth in the upper jaw are visible

Crocodile

Alligator

Lizards

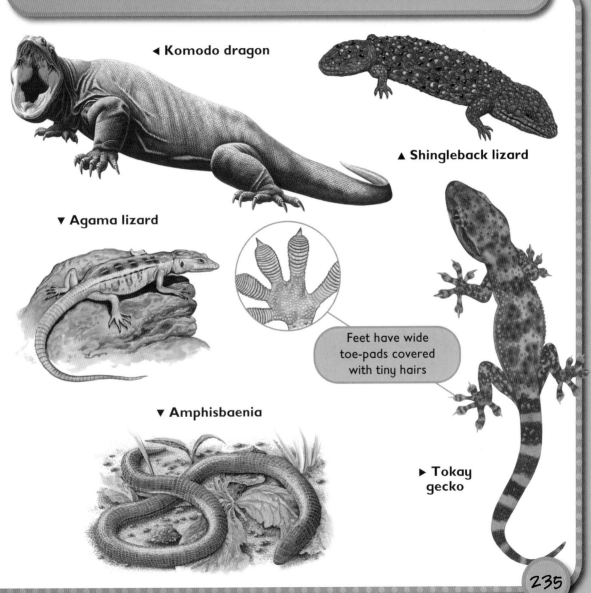

◀ **Komodo dragon**

▲ **Shingleback lizard**

▼ **Agama lizard**

Feet have wide
toe-pads covered
with tiny hairs

▼ **Amphisbaenia**

▶ **Tokay
gecko**

Lizards

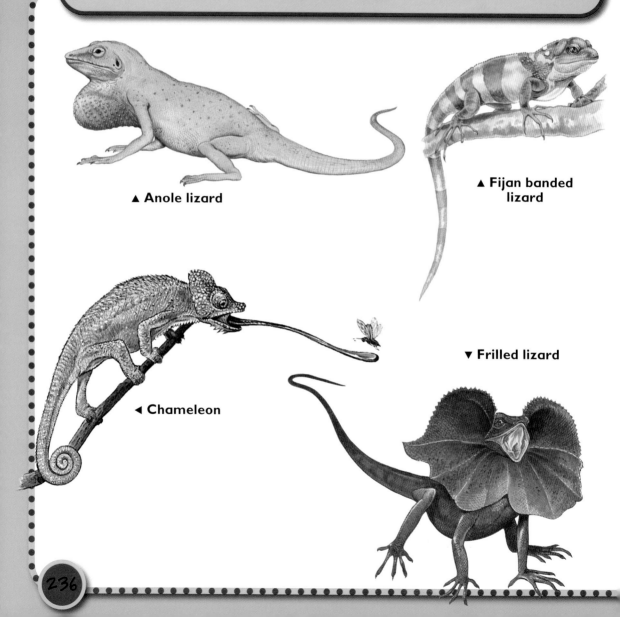

▲ Anole lizard

▲ Fijan banded lizard

◄ Chameleon

▼ Frilled lizard

◀ Six-lined
racerunner

◀ Crested water
dragon

▼ Gecko

▼ Chuckwalla lizard

◀ Gila monster

237

Snake anatomy

▶ Organs

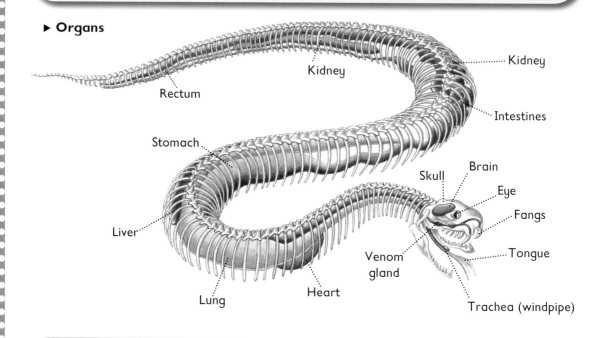

Kidney

Kidney

Rectum

Intestines

Stomach

Skull

Brain

Eye

Fangs

Liver

Tongue

Venom gland

Lung

Heart

Trachea (windpipe)

Fang position

Primitive snakes
Heavy skulls with a short
lower jaw and few teeth

Rear-fanged snakes
Fangs are positioned in
the roof of their mouths

Front-fanged snakes
Fangs are positioned at
the front of their mouths

▼ **Jaws**

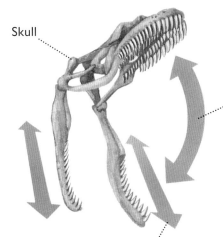

Skull

Lower jaws can detach from the skull to accommodate larger prey

Lower jaws work independently, with first one side pulling and then the other, to draw prey into the throat

Folding fangs

Venom gland

Tube for injecting venom

▲ **Venom**

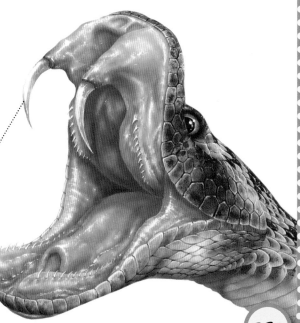

Venom runs down the groove on the outside of the fangs and is injected into the victim's body

▶ **Rattlesnake**

239

Snakes

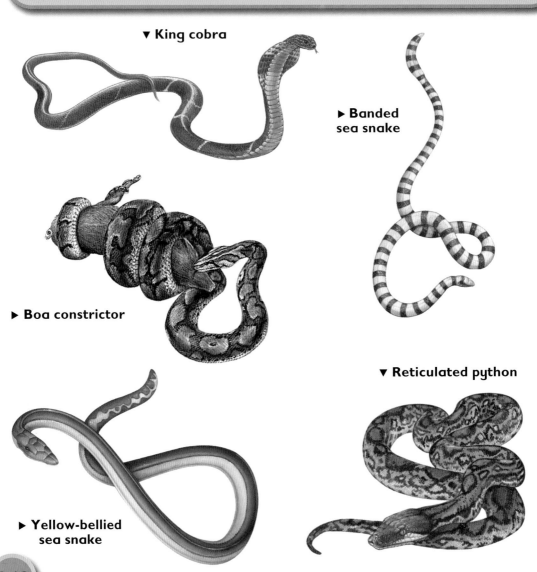

▼ **King cobra**

▶ **Banded sea snake**

▶ **Boa constrictor**

▼ **Reticulated python**

▶ **Yellow-bellied sea snake**

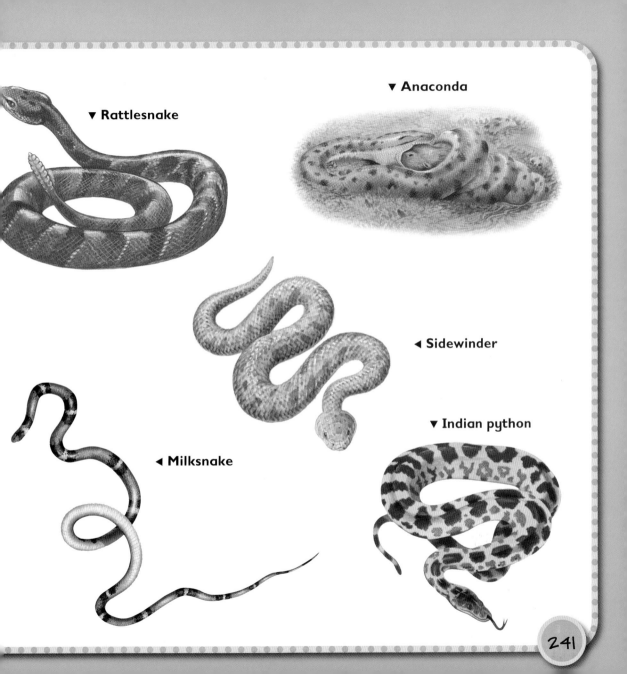

▼ Anaconda

▼ Rattlesnake

◄ Sidewinder

▼ Indian python

◄ Milksnake

241

▼ **Anatomy**

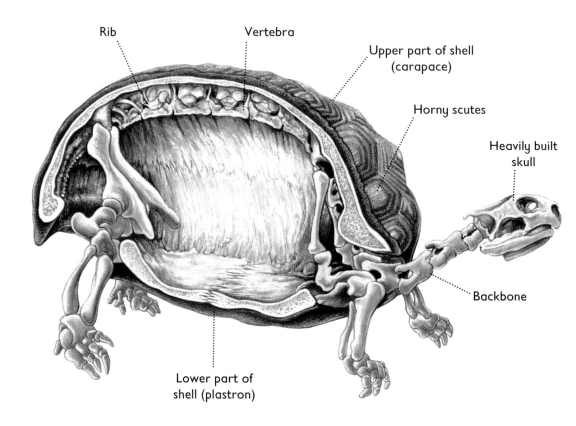

Rib

Vertebra

Upper part of shell
(carapace)

Horny scutes

Heavily built
skull

Backbone

Lower part of
shell (plastron)

▲ Giant tortoise

▲ Leopard tortoise

▶ Desert tortoise

243

Turtles

▼ Snapping turtle

▲ Indian soft shell turtle

▼ Green turtle

▲ Mata mata turtle

◄ **Hawksbill turtle**

▼ **Pacific Ridley turtle**

▲ **Leatherback turtle**

▼ **Loggerhead turtle hatchlings**
Turtle hatchlings must make their way quickly to the safety of the water.

▼ **Green turtle nest**
Females return to the beach where they were born to dig their nest. After they have laid their eggs, they return to the water.

Bird anatomy

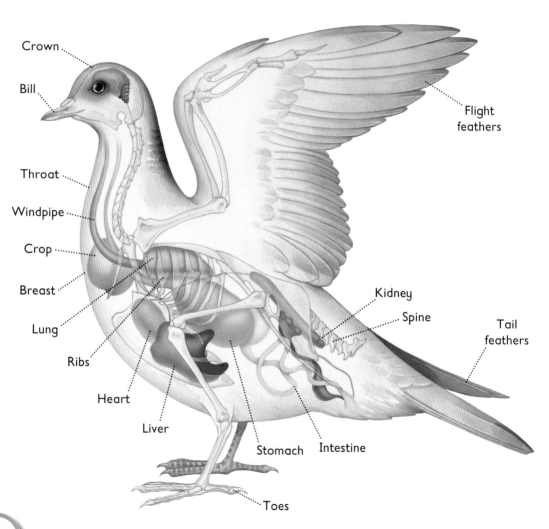

Crown

Bill

Throat

Windpipe

Crop

Breast

Lung

Ribs

Heart

Liver

Stomach

Intestine

Kidney

Spine

Flight feathers

Tail feathers

Toes

Feet varieties

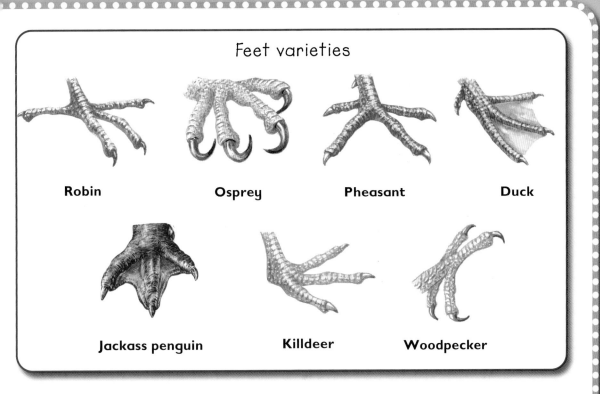

Robin

Osprey

Pheasant

Duck

Jackass penguin

Killdeer

Woodpecker

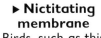

▶ **Nictitating membrane**
Birds, such as this barking owl, have a clear third eyelid called the nictitating membrane.

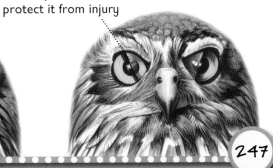

Membrane moves across eye to keep it clean and to protect it from injury

Feathers and flight

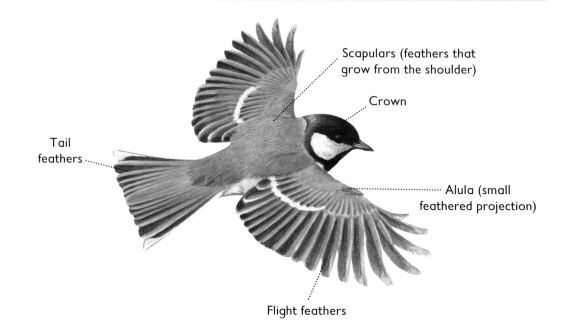

Scapulars (feathers that grow from the shoulder)

Crown

Tail feathers

Alula (small feathered projection)

Flight feathers

▼ How birds fly
In flight, a bird's flapping wings make circular up-and-down movements.

Feather varieties

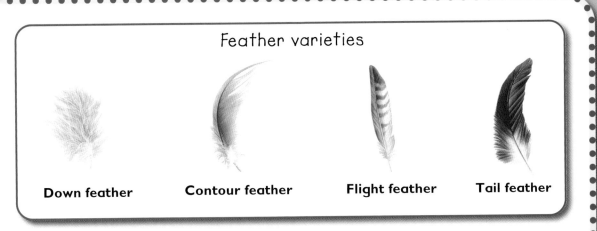

Down feather   **Contour feather**   **Flight feather**   **Tail feather**

▼ Cold-climate feathers
A layer of short feathers lie next to a penguin's skin. The longer top feathers overlap to trap warm air, or separate to allow it to escape.

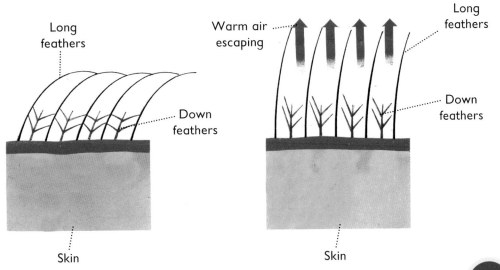

Long feathers

Down feathers

Skin

Warm air escaping

Long feathers

Down feathers

Skin

Eggs and nests

▼ Weaver bird

2. Then he makes the roof and the entrance

3. When he's finished, the long entrance helps to provide a safe shelter for the eggs

1. The male Weaver bird twists strips of leaves around a twig

◄ Cave swiftlet

·············· Nest made of feathers and grass, stuck together with the bird's saliva

▼ Gentoo penguin
Male Gentoo penguins offer their females pebbles for building a large nest, which will protect their two eggs.

Egg varieties

Jacana

Hedge sparrow

Cetti's warbler

Quail

Blue jay

Common snipe

Auk

Scarlet tanager

Catbird

House wren

▼ Hatching

1. The chick starts to chip away at the egg

2. The chick uses its egg tooth to break free

3. The egg splits wide open

4. The chick is able to wriggle free

Penguins

▲ Emperor

▲ Rockhopper

▶ Adelie

▶ King

▲ Macaroni

▲ Royal

◄ Chinstrap

◄ Gentoo

Penguins

▲ Snares

▶ Yellow-eyed

◀ Jackass

◀ Erect-crested

◄ **Magellanic**

▲ **Peruvian**

▼ **Galapagos**

▲ **Little**

► **Fjordland**

Water birds

▲ Sanderling

◀ Knot

▲ Avocet

▲ Purple sandpiper

▲ Bar-tailed godwit

▶ Oystercatcher

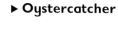

▲ Lapwing

256

▼ Stone curlew

▲ Ringed plover

▲ Curlew

► Dunlin

◄ Grey plover

▲ Turnstone

Water birds

◄ **Golden plover**

▲ **Red shank**

► **Bittern**

◄ **Flamingo**

◄ **Grey heron**

▶ **Razorbill**

▶ **African jacana**

▼ **Courser**

◀ **Wrybill**

▶ **Guillemot**

◀ **Puffin**

Water birds

▶ **Brent goose**

◀ **Pink-footed goose**

▲ **Scaup**

▼ **Eider**

▶ **Shelduck**

▲ Common scoter

▼ Red-breasted merganser

▼ Swan

Water birds

◄ Manx
shearwater

◄ Fulmar

▼ Red-footed
boobie

▼ Blue-footed
boobie

► Diving
gannet

▲ Albatross

▼ Mediterranean gull

► Little tern

▼ Cormorant

◄ Frigate bird

263

Water birds

◀ Great skua

▶ Pomarine skua

◀ Common gull

◀ Common tern

◀ Arctic skua

▶ Arctic tern

▲ Glaucus gull

◀ Sandwich tern

▼ Black-headed gull

▶ Black skimmer

265

▶ **Herring gull**

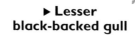

▶ **Lesser black-backed gull**

▼ **Kittiwake**

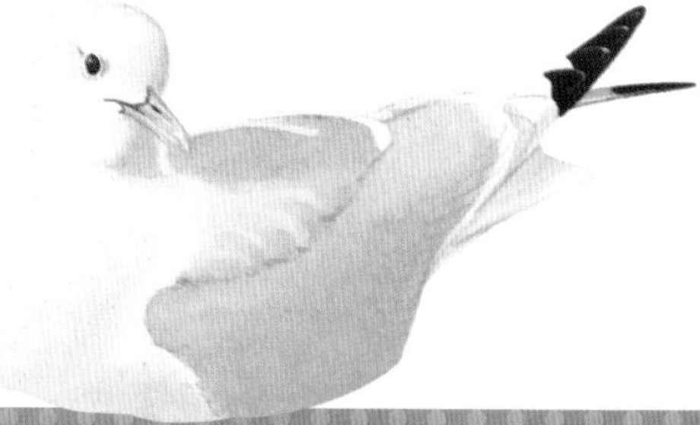

▲ **Great black-backed gull**

Birds of prey

▶ Sparrowhawk

▶ Lappet vulture

▼ Peregrine falcon

▶ Bald eagle

▶ Collared falconet

Birds of prey

▼ Golden eagle

▶ Osprey

▶ Harpy eagle

▼ Egyptian vulture

◀ Snail kite

Game birds

▶ Pheasant

◀ Sandgrouse

▼ Peacock

▼ Partridge

◀ Mallee

269

Pigeons and doves

◄ Passenger pigeon

◄ Feral pigeon

▼ White dove

▶ Turtle dove

◄ Stock dove

◄ Rock dove

Owls

▲ **Little owl**

► **Brown fish owl**

Feathery tufts on head

▼ **Barn owl**

◄ **Great horned owl**

Owls

◀ Boobook owl

▶ Scops owl

◀ Tawny owl

◀ Elf owl

272

Woodpeckers

▼ **Green woodpecker**

◄ **Great spotted woodpecker**

► **Acorn woodpecker**

► **Eurasion woodpecker**

◄ **Lesser spotted woodpecker**

◄ **Sapsucker**

Perching birds

▼ Mountain chickadee

▲ American robin

▲ Shore lark

▶ Crossbill

◀ Snow bunting

▶ Cactus wren

◄ Blackbird

▲ Chaffinch

▲ Waxwing

◄ Antbird

▼ Nuthatch

► Chough

275

Perching birds

▶ Jay

◀ Mistle thrush

▶ Redwing

▼ Garden warbler

▶ Raven

▲ Reed bunting

276

▶ Dunnock

▼ Wren

▶ Lyre bird

▼ Song thrush

◀ Rock pipet

277

Perching birds

▶ Goldcrest

▶ Fairy wren

◀ Rook

▶ Spotted flycatcher

▶ Long-tailed tit

▶ Magpie

◀ Goldfinch

▶ Jackdaw

▼ Bullfinch

▶ Carrion crow

▲ Chiffchaff

279

▼ Blackcap

◄ Fieldfare

◄ House martin

▲ Brambling

▲ Pied wagtail

▼ Manakin

◀ Swallow

▶ Rufous hornero

▶ Mockingbird

▶ Treecreeper

281

Monotremes and marsupials

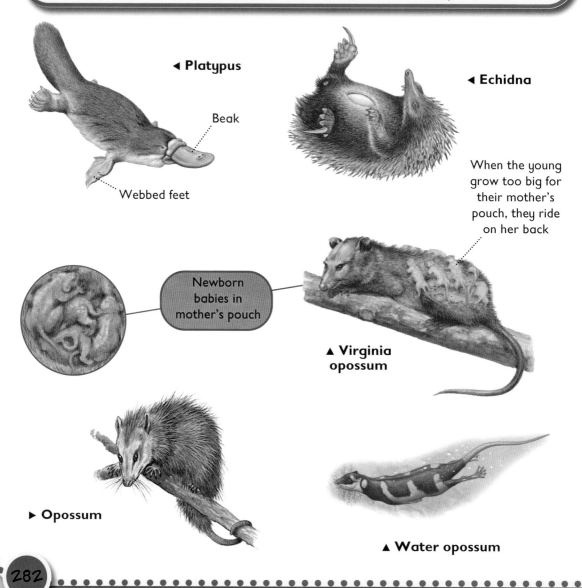

◀ Platypus

Beak

Webbed feet

◀ Echidna

When the young grow too big for their mother's pouch, they ride on her back

Newborn babies in mother's pouch

▲ Virginia opossum

▶ Opossum

▲ Water opossum

◄ **Koala**

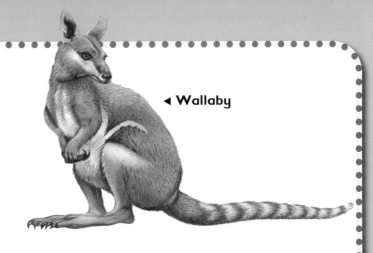

◄ **Wallaby**

3. Within six months, the joey has grown enough to feed outside the pouch

2. A joey suckling on its mother's teat

1. Newborn joeys climbing up their mother's belly to her pouch

► **Kangaroo**

Bats

▶ **Pipistrelle bat**

◀ **Fruit bat**

Up close

Pipistrelle

Flying fox

Vampire bat

Horseshoe bat

▲ **Blossom bat**

▼ Echolocation
Bats hunt in darkness by sending out
high-pitched bursts of sound. If another
animal is close, the sound bounces back off
its body, allowing the bat to locate its prey.

▲ **False
vampire bat**

Primates

▲ Dusky titi

▼ Howler monkey

▼ Mandrill

▶ Barbary ape

▼ Chimpanzee

▶ Baboon

◀ White-cheeked mangabey

▼ Orang-utan

▶ Golden lion tamarin

Moles, hedgehogs and shrews

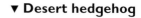
▼ Desert hedgehog

▲ Mole

▶ European hedgehog

▼ Pygmy shrew

▲ Tree shrew

Rabbits, hares and pikas

▼ Rabbit

◄ Brown hare

▲ Arctic hare

▶ Pika

Rodents

◀ **African gerbil**

▼ **Porcupine**

▶ **Capybara**

▲ **Pocket gopher**

▶ **Naked mole rat**

▲ **Kangaroo rat**

◀ **Red squirrel**

▲ **Grey squirrel**

▶ **Field vole**

▼ **Burrowing house mouse**

◀ **Field mouse**

▲ **Harvest mouse**

Whales

▼ **Skeleton**

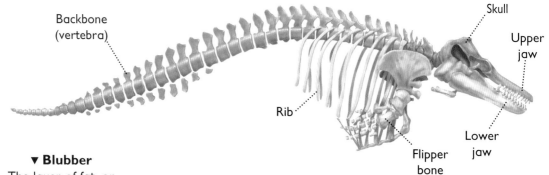

Backbone (vertebra)

Skull

Upper jaw

Rib

Flipper bone

Lower jaw

▼ **Blubber**
The layer of fat, or blubber, under a whale's skin is five times thicker than the layer of fat beneath a human's skin.

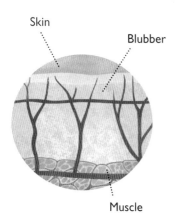

Skin

Blubber

Muscle

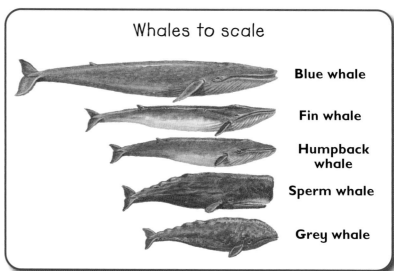

Whales to scale

Blue whale

Fin whale

Humpback whale

Sperm whale

Grey whale

▼ Bowhead whale

▲ Blue whale

▼ White whale

▲ Sperm whale

▼ Narwhals

▲ Grey whale

293

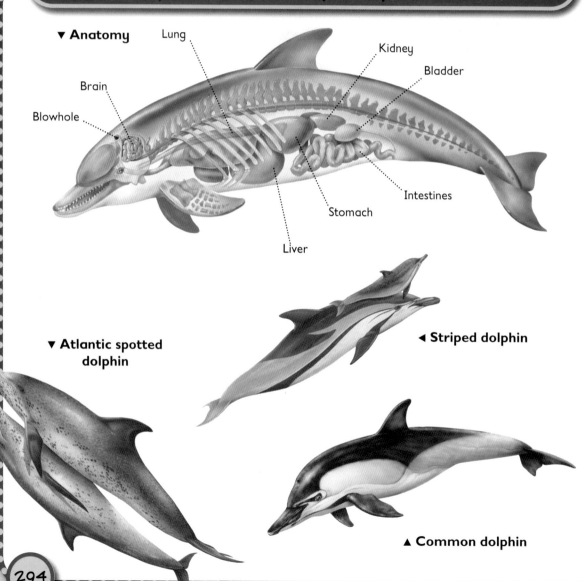

▼ **Anatomy**

Lung

Kidney

Bladder

Brain

Blowhole

Intestines

Stomach

Liver

▼ **Atlantic spotted dolphin**

◀ **Striped dolphin**

▲ **Common dolphin**

▲ Bottlenose dolphin

▶ Finless porpoise

▲ Harbour porpoise

▲ Killer whale

▼ Spectacled porpoise

▶ Dall's porpoise

Dog anatomy

▼ **Skeleton**

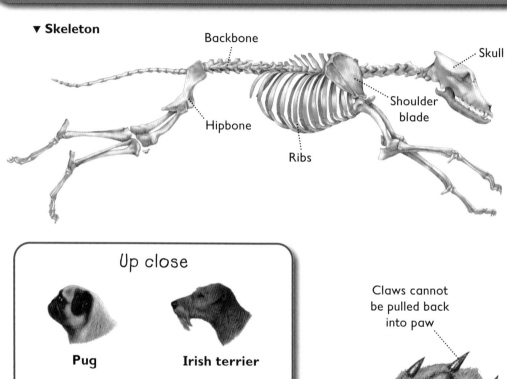

Backbone

Skull

Hipbone

Shoulder blade

Ribs

Up close

Pug

Irish terrier

Great Dane

Grey wolf

Claws cannot be pulled back into paw

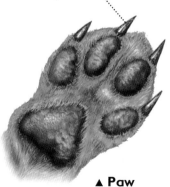

▲ **Paw**

Wild dogs

▼ Dingo

▼ Red fox

▼ Jackal

► Coyote

◄ Grey wolf

▼ Grey fox

Domestic dogs

▼ Basset hound

▲ Pointer

▶ Chow Chow

▼ Golden retriever

▲ Afghan hound

▲ Chinese
crested dog

▶ Siberian
husky

▲ Bloodhound

▼ Poodle

▶ Pyrenean
mountain dog

299

Bears

▶ Giant panda

▲ Sun bear

▼ Grizzly bear

▲ Polar bear

▲ Sloth bear

▼ Kodiak bear

▲ Spectacled bear

▼ Black bear

Mustelids

▶ Eurasian otter

▼ Stoat

▲ Polecat

▼ Skunk

◀ Badger

▲ Weasel

Civets and mongooses

◀ **Cusimanse mongoose**

▶ **Celebes palm civet**

▼ **Meerkat**

Cat anatomy

▼ Skeleton

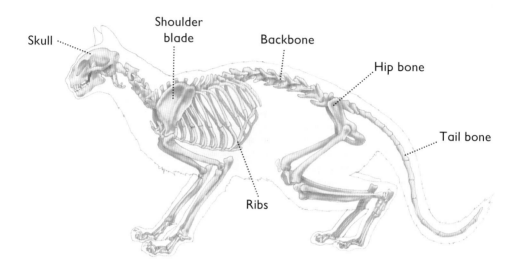

Skull

Shoulder blade

Backbone

Hip bone

Tail bone

Ribs

▼ Tongue

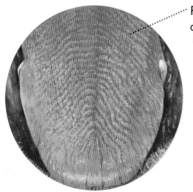

Papillae — bumps on the surface of the tongue that help grip food while the teeth are chewing

▼ Fur

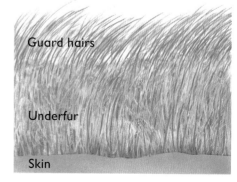

Guard hairs

Underfur

Skin

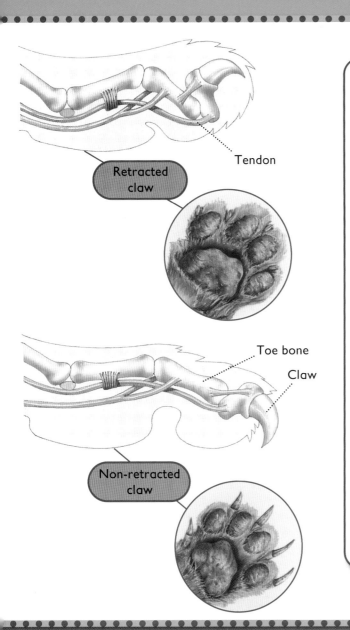

Tendon

Retracted claw

Toe bone

Claw

Non-retracted claw

Pupil closed

Bright daylight
The cat's pupil narrows to a slit, allowing less daylight in.

Pupil open

Darkness
The pupil widens to let in as much light as possible.

Nictitating membrane

Nictitating membrane
A cat has a 'third eyelid', or nictitating membrane. This can move partly across to protect the eye.

Wild cats

◄ Puma

▲ Caracal

► Cheetah

▼ Leopard

► Clouded leopard

▼ Jaguar

▲ Snow leopard

◄ Tiger

◄ Serval

◄ Lion

◄ Lynx

307

Domestic cats

◀ **Siamese**

▼ **British blue**

▲ **Abyssinian**

▶ **Scottish fold**

▶ **Japanese bobtail**

◄ Maine coon

▲ Sphynx

► Manx

▼ American curl

◄ Persian

Elephants

▲ African elephant

▲ Asian elephant

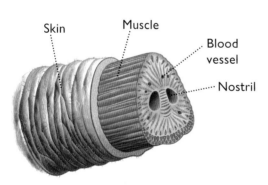

Skin

Muscle

Blood vessel

Nostril

▲ Inside a trunk

▲ African elephant trunk

▲ Asian elephant trunk

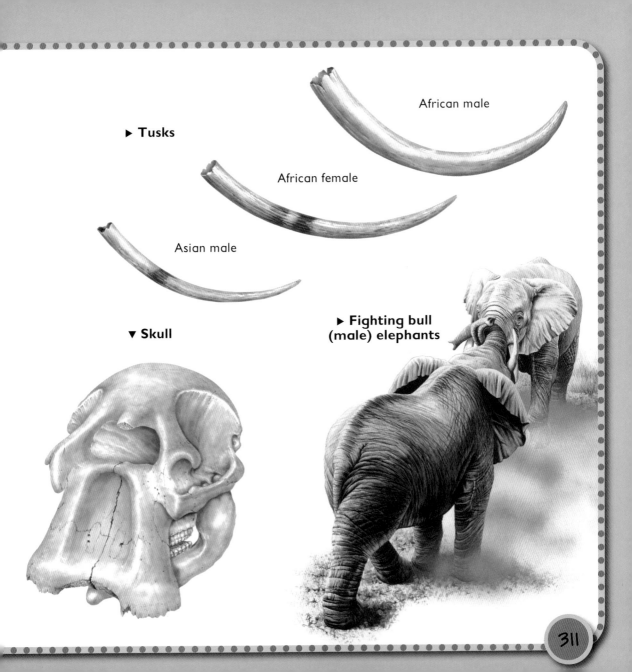

▶ **Tusks**

African male

African female

Asian male

▼ **Skull**

▶ **Fighting bull (male) elephants**

Hoofed mammals

▼ Red deer

▲ Roe deer

▼ Reindeer

► Caribou

◀ **White rhinoceros**

▲ **Black rhinoceros**

▶ **Bactrian camel**

▶ **Dromedary camel**

◀ **Giraffe**

◀ **Okapi**

313

Horse anatomy

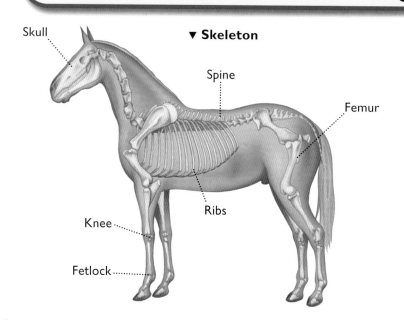

Skull

▼ Skeleton

Spine

Femur

Ribs

Knee

Fetlock

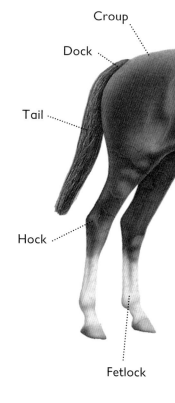

Croup

Dock

Tail

Hock

Fetlock

► Hoof

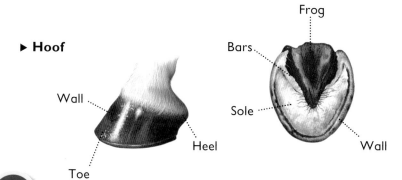

Frog

Bars

Wall

Sole

Heel

Toe

Wall

▼ **Points
of a horse**

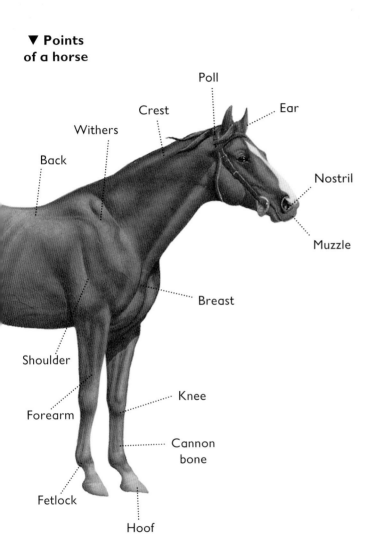

Poll

Crest

Ear

Withers

Back

Nostril

Muzzle

Breast

Shoulder

Knee

Forearm

Cannon
bone

Fetlock

Hoof

Markings

Star

Stripe

White face

Blaze

Snip

Gaits

▼ Walk

▼ Trot

▼ Canter

▼ Gallop

Horse family

▲ Shetland pony

▲ Fell pony

▶ Connemara pony

▶ Pinto pony

Horse family

◄ Arab

▲ Morgan

► Lipizzaner

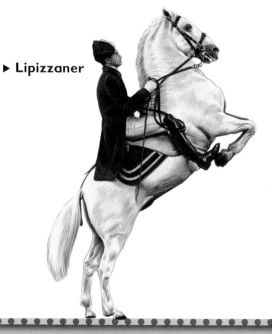

◄ Shire

▲ Przewalski's horse

▼ Arab

◄ Zebra

Stripe patterns

Grevy's zebra

Burchell's zebra

Mountain zebra

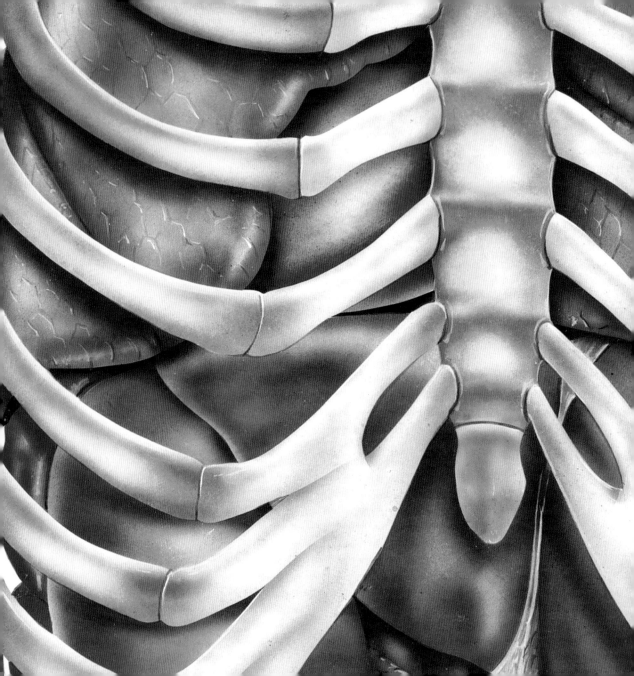

Human Body

Inside a cell

Cell membrane
A thin layer of protein
and fat surrounds the cell

Mitochondria
Release energy by breaking
down sugars in the blood

Nucleus
The cell's
control centre

Golgi bodies
Send chemicals to parts
of the body where they
are needed

Cytoplasm
A jelly-like liquid
fills the cell

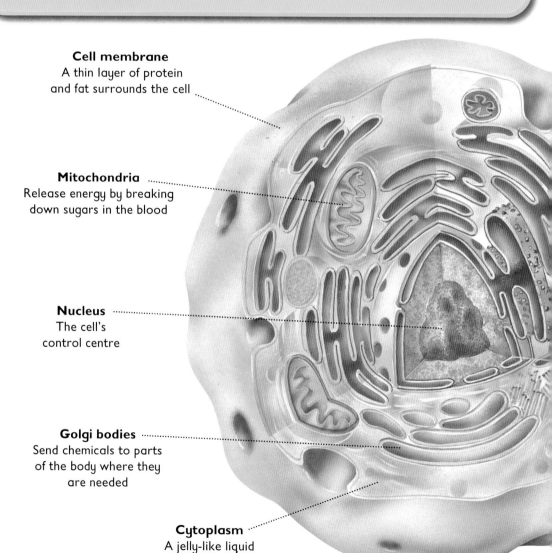

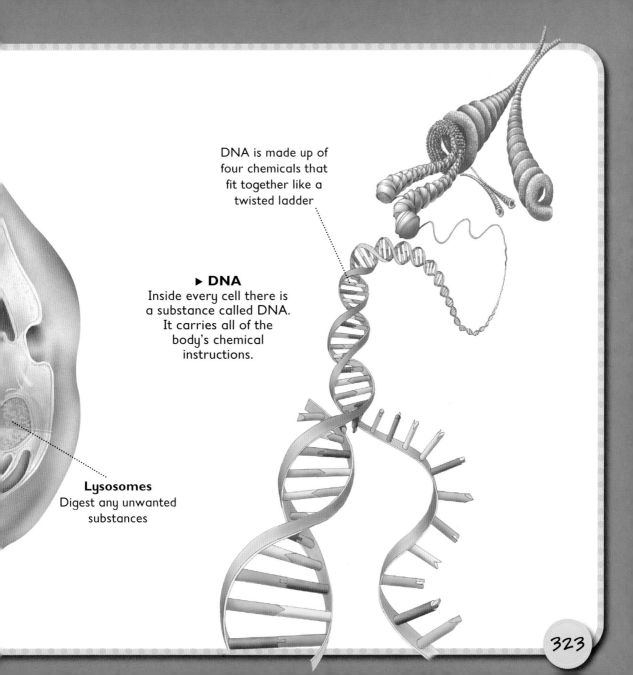

DNA is made up of
four chemicals that
fit together like a
twisted ladder

▶ **DNA**
Inside every cell there is
a substance called DNA.
It carries all of the
body's chemical
instructions.

Lysosomes
Digest any unwanted
substances

323

Blood

▶ Blood vessels

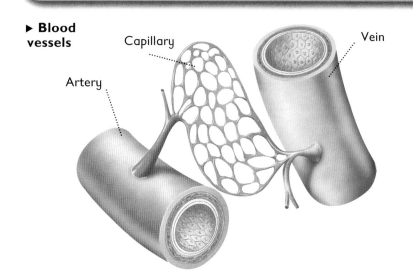

Capillary

Vein

Artery

▼ Granulocytes
These blood cells clean the blood by eating germs.

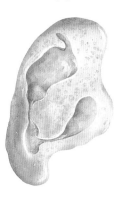

▼ Inside a blood vessel

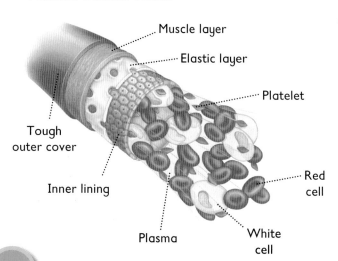

Muscle layer

Elastic layer

Platelet

Tough outer cover

Inner lining

Red cell

Plasma

White cell

▲ Red blood cells
Carry oxygen around the body.

▼ Platelets
In order to stop bleeding, platelets are cells that enable blood to clot.

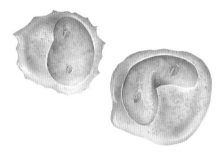

Carotid artery

Heart

Blood vessels in lung

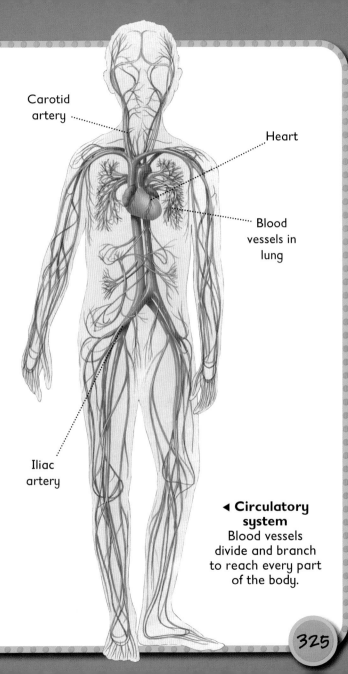

Iliac artery

▲ Eosinophils and basophils
These blood cells help fight off disease.

◄ Circulatory system
Blood vessels divide and branch to reach every part of the body.

Inside the heart

KEY

1. Aorta
2. Pulmonary artery
3. Right atrium
4. Tricuspid valve
5. Right ventricle
6. Pulmonary valve
7. Left atrium
8. Mitral valve
9. Left ventricle
10. Superior vena cava
11. Inferior vena cava
12. Pulmonary vein

Location

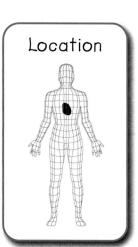

From upper body

To upper body

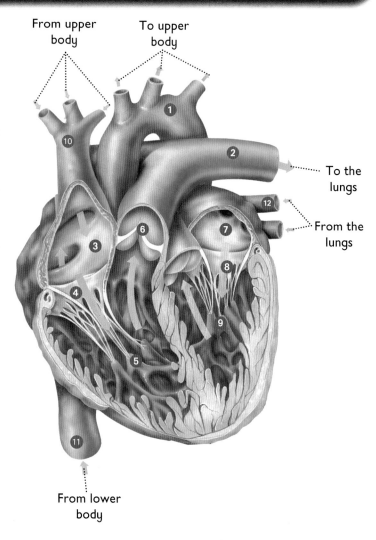

To the lungs

From the lungs

From lower body

Heartbeat

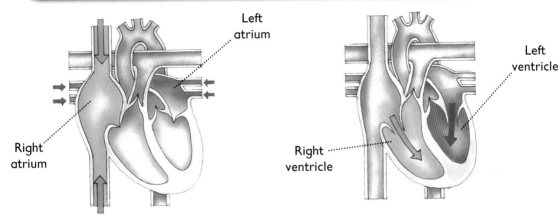

Left atrium

Right atrium

1. Upper chambers fill with blood

Left ventricle

Right ventricle

2. Blood passes through valves into lower chambers

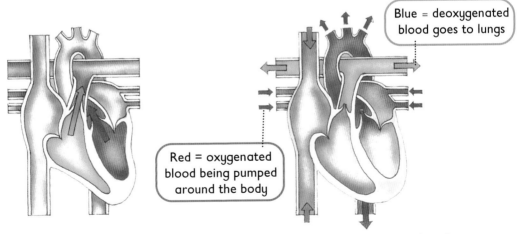

Blue = deoxygenated blood goes to lungs

Red = oxygenated blood being pumped around the body

3. The lower chambers contract, pushing blood into the arteries

4. Blood starts to fill up the relaxed upper chambers from the veins

Respiratory system

▶ Lungs

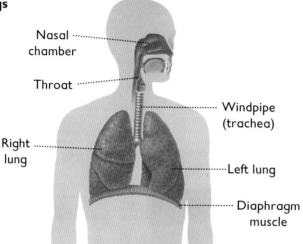

- Nasal chamber
- Throat
- Windpipe (trachea)
- Right lung
- Left lung
- Diaphragm muscle

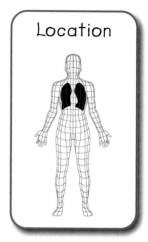

Location

▶ Inhalation

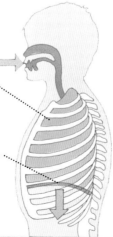

The muscles between the ribs expand, inflating the lungs

The diaphragm flattens, pulling the lungs down and sucking air in

▶ Exhalation

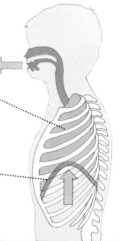

The muscles between the ribs relax, letting the lungs deflate

The diaphragm arches up, pushing air out of the lungs

Lungs

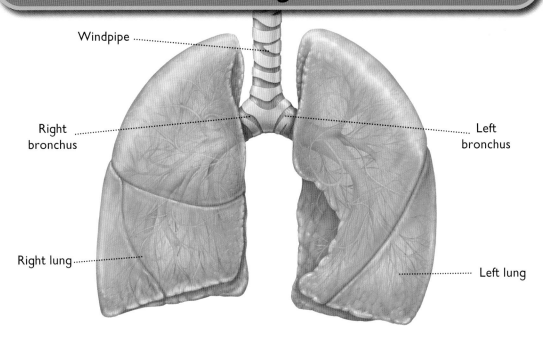

Windipe

Right bronchus

Left bronchus

Right lung

Left lung

▼ Inside the bronchi

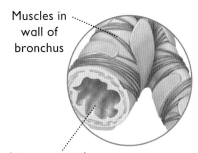

Muscles in wall of bronchus

Air space inside bronchus

▼ Alveoli

The bronchi divide into smaller bronchioles. At the end of each bronchiole is a group of tiny air sacs called alveoli.

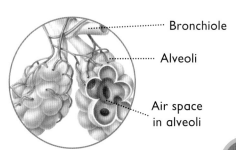

Bronchiole

Alveoli

Air space in alveoli

Digestive system

Location

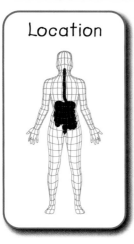

▶ **Swallowing**

1. Tongue presses food to the back of the mouth

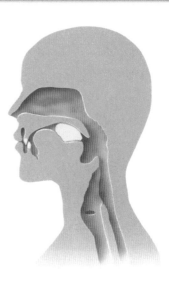

2. Food passes over the top of the windpipe

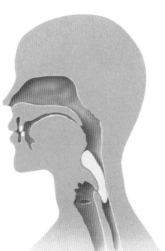

3. Food is pushed down the gullet

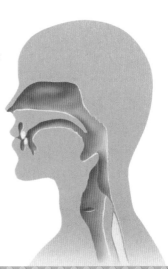

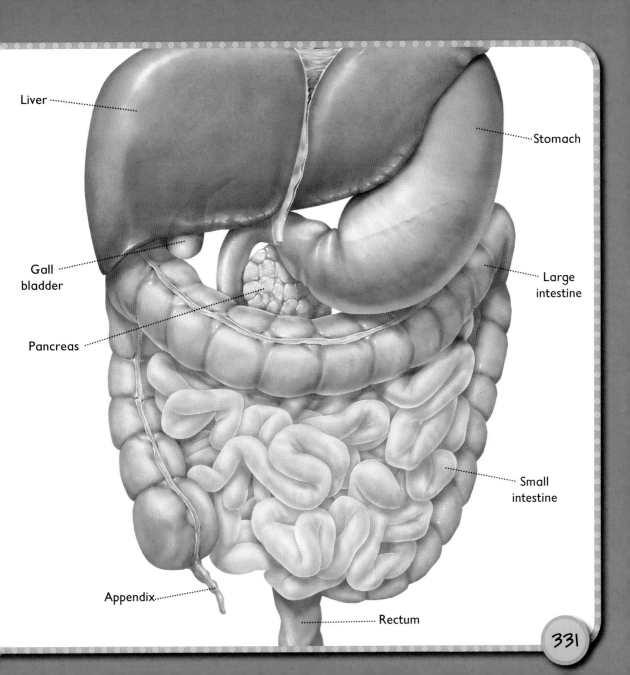

Liver

Stomach

Gall
bladder

Large
intestine

Pancreas

Small
intestine

Appendix

Rectum

331

Urinary system

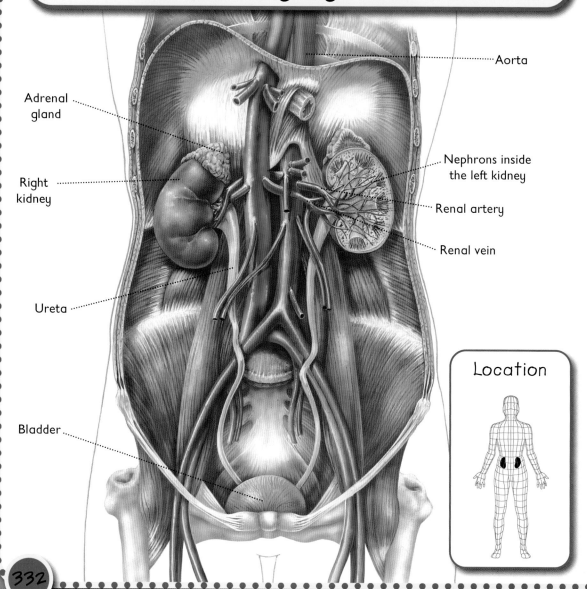

Aorta

Adrenal gland

Right kidney

Nephrons inside the left kidney

Renal artery

Renal vein

Ureta

Bladder

Location

Reproductive system

▶ **Female reproductive system**

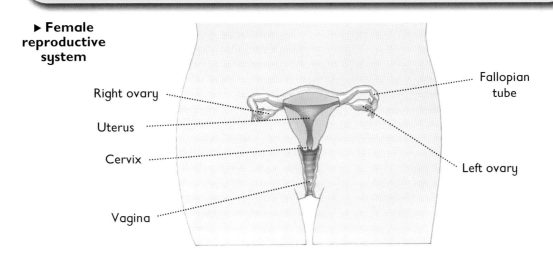

Right ovary

Uterus

Cervix

Vagina

Fallopian tube

Left ovary

▼ **Sperm cell**

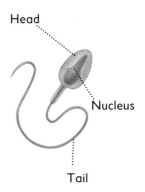

Head

Nucleus

Tail

▶ **Male reproductive system**

Bladder

Urethra

Testes

Penis

Baby development

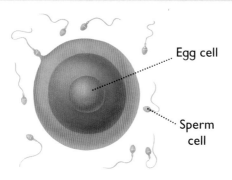

Egg cell

Sperm cell

▲ Fertilization
A single sperm cell fertilizes the female egg cell.

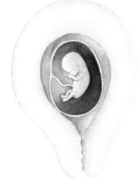

8 weeks
Main organs are formed.

20 weeks
Hair begins to grow.

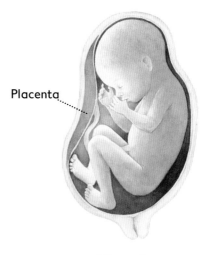

Placenta

32 weeks
Fat collects under skin.

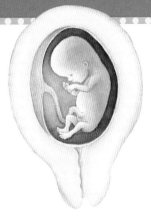

12 weeks
Heart beats, and kicking
movements begin.

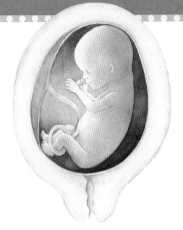

16 weeks
Foetus now so big that the
mother's abdomen starts to bulge.

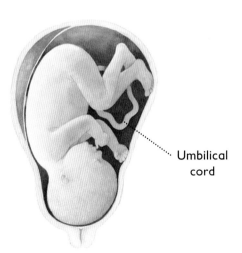

Umbilical
cord

36 weeks
Baby turns head down.

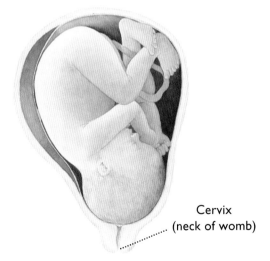

Cervix
(neck of womb)

40 weeks
Ready for birth.

Skeleton

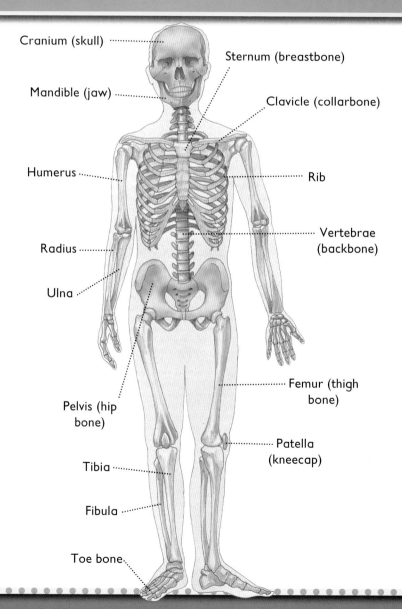

Cranium (skull)

Mandible (jaw)

Humerus

Radius

Ulna

Pelvis (hip bone)

Tibia

Fibula

Toe bone

Sternum (breastbone)

Clavicle (collarbone)

Rib

Vertebrae (backbone)

Femur (thigh bone)

Patella (kneecap)

Bones and joints

▶ **Inside a bone**

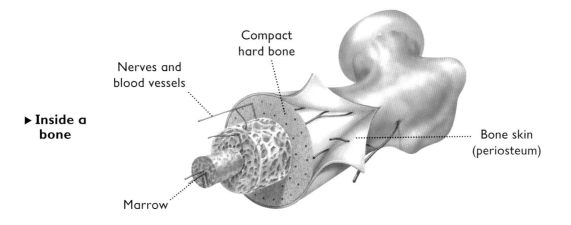

Nerves and blood vessels

Compact hard bone

Bone skin (periosteum)

Marrow

▼ **Shoulder joint**

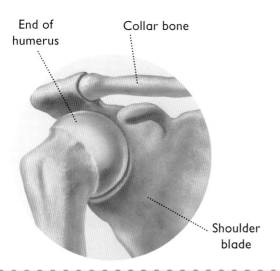

End of humerus

Collar bone

Shoulder blade

▼ **Knee joint**

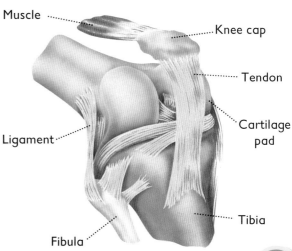

Muscle

Knee cap

Tendon

Cartilage pad

Ligament

Fibula

Tibia

Muscles

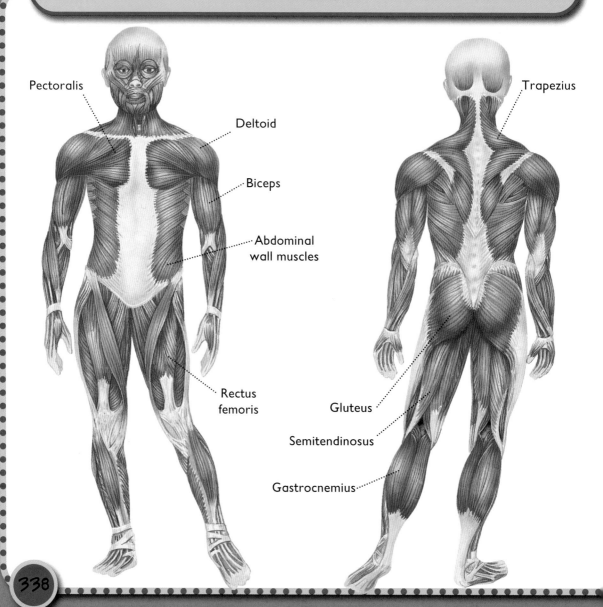

Pectoralis

Deltoid

Biceps

Abdominal
wall muscles

Rectus
femoris

Trapezius

Gluteus

Semitendinosus

Gastrocnemius

▶ Inside a muscle

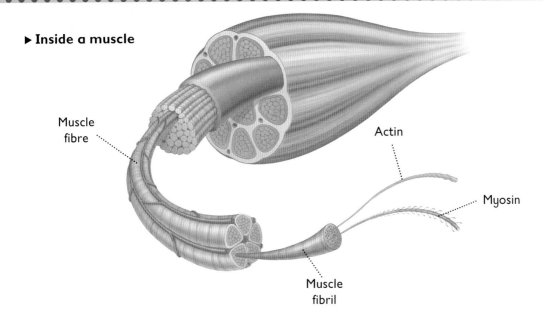

Muscle fibre

Actin

Myosin

Muscle fibril

▼ How muscles work

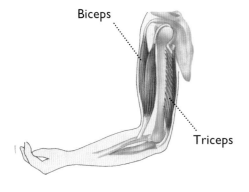

Biceps

Triceps

Biceps get shorter and the elbow moves

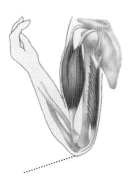

To move the arm back down, the triceps shortens and the biceps gets longer

Skin, hair and nails

▼ **Inside the skin**

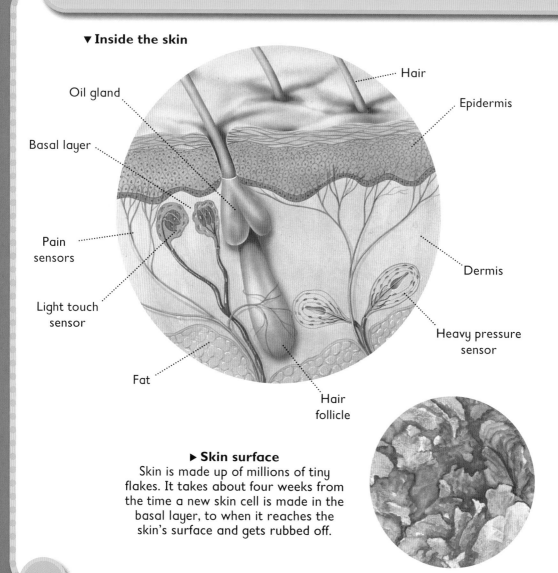

Hair

Epidermis

Oil gland

Basal layer

Pain sensors

Light touch sensor

Fat

Hair follicle

Dermis

Heavy pressure sensor

▶ **Skin surface**
Skin is made up of millions of tiny flakes. It takes about four weeks from the time a new skin cell is made in the basal layer, to when it reaches the skin's surface and gets rubbed off.

Hair types

Black curly hair

Blonde wavy hair

Straight black hair

Straight red hair

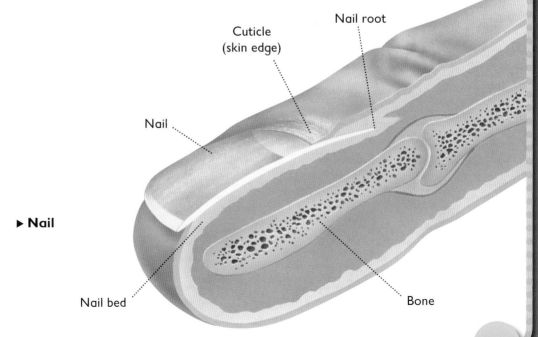

Cuticle (skin edge)

Nail root

Nail

Nail bed

Bone

▶ **Nail**

Brain

▼ Inside the brain

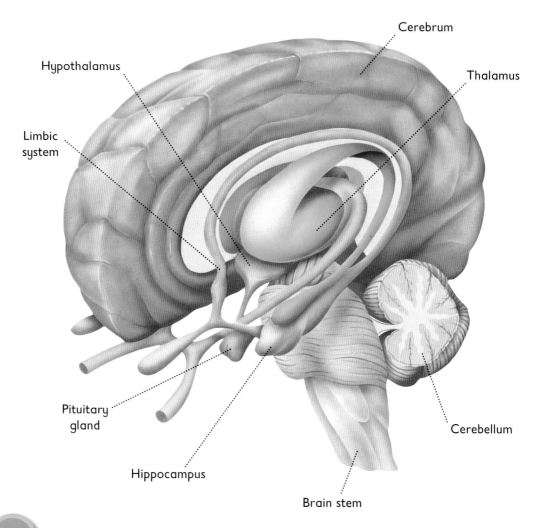

Cerebrum

Thalamus

Hypothalamus

Limbic system

Pituitary gland

Hippocampus

Brain stem

Cerebellum

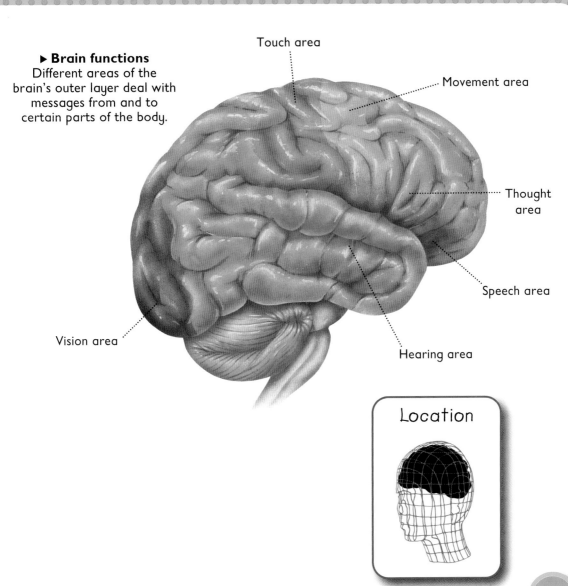

▶ Brain functions
Different areas of the
brain's outer layer deal with
messages from and to
certain parts of the body.

Touch area

Movement area

Thought
area

Speech area

Vision area

Hearing area

Location

Sight

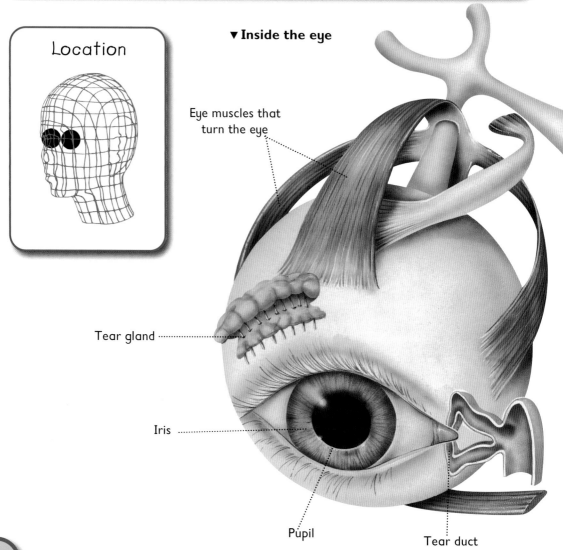

Location

▼ **Inside the eye**

Eye muscles that
turn the eye

Tear gland

Iris

Pupil

Tear duct

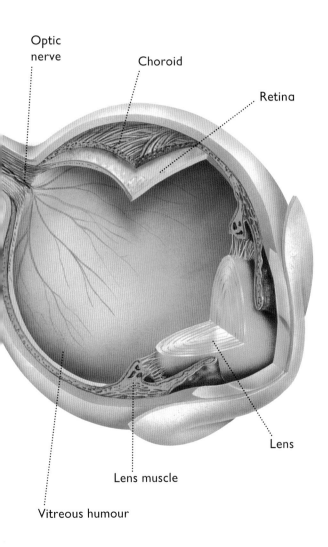

Optic nerve

Choroid

Retina

Lens

Lens muscle

Vitreous humour

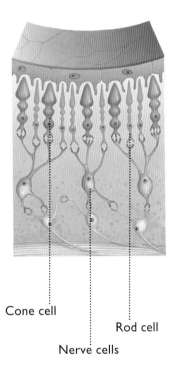

Cone cell

Rod cell

Nerve cells

▲ Inside the retina
Cone and rod cells trigger signals in nerve cells, which then get sent to the brain.

Hearing and speaking

How loud?

Volume is measured in decibels (dB)

Whisper 20 dB

Ordinary speech 60 dB

Loud appliance 75 dB

Motorcycle 100 dB

Jet engine 130 dB

▼ **Inside the ear**

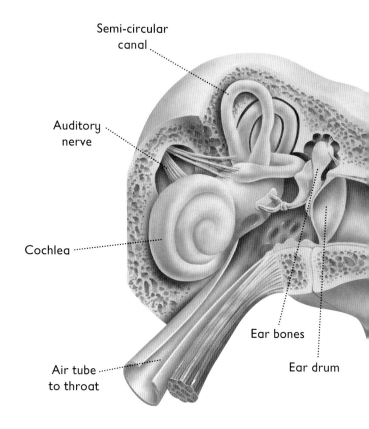

Semi-circular canal

Auditory nerve

Cochlea

Air tube to throat

Ear bones

Ear drum

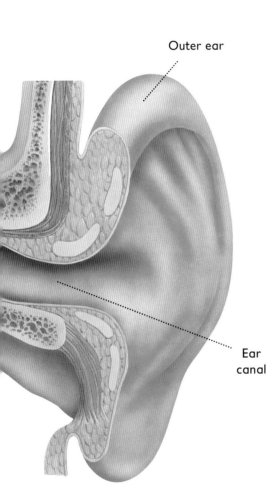

Outer ear

Ear
canal

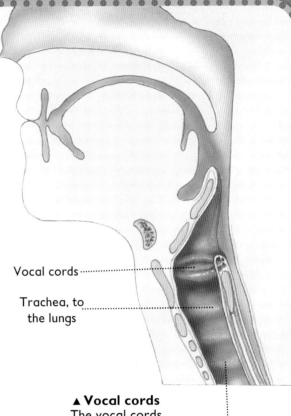

Vocal cords

Trachea, to
the lungs

Throat

▲ **Vocal cords**
The vocal cords
are held apart for
breathing and pulled
together for speech.

Taste and smell

▶ **Tongue**

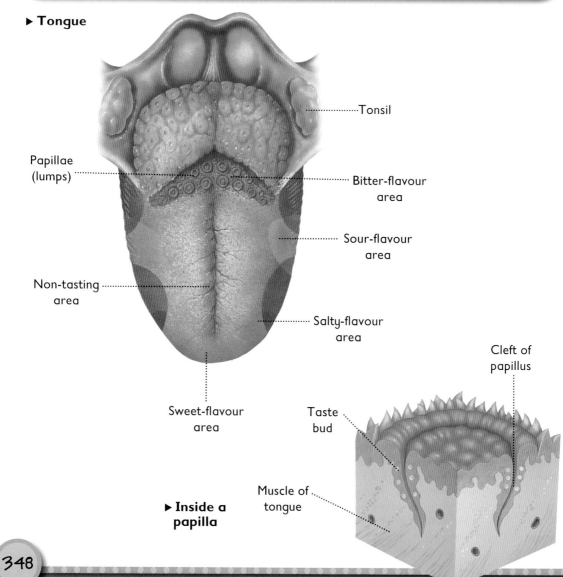

Tonsil

Papillae (lumps)

Bitter-flavour area

Sour-flavour area

Non-tasting area

Salty-flavour area

Sweet-flavour area

Cleft of papillus

Taste bud

Muscle of tongue

▶ **Inside a papilla**

▶ Nasal cavity

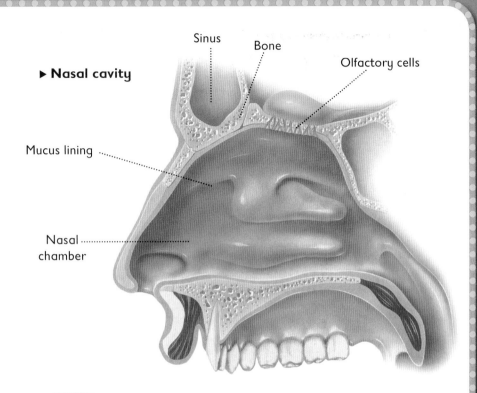

Sinus

Bone

Olfactory cells

Mucus lining

Nasal chamber

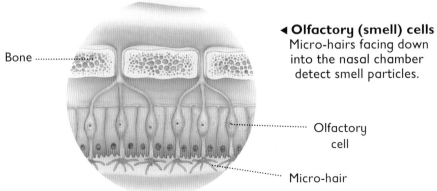

Bone

◀ Olfactory (smell) cells
Micro-hairs facing down into the nasal chamber detect smell particles.

Olfactory cell

Micro-hair

Nerves

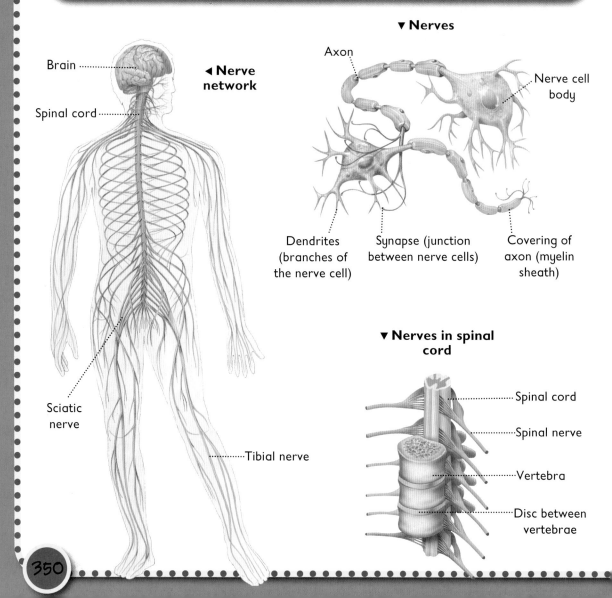

Brain

Spinal cord

◀ **Nerve network**

Sciatic nerve

Tibial nerve

▼ **Nerves**

Axon

Nerve cell body

Dendrites (branches of the nerve cell)

Synapse (junction between nerve cells)

Covering of axon (myelin sheath)

▼ **Nerves in spinal cord**

Spinal cord

Spinal nerve

Vertebra

Disc between vertebrae

Hormones

▼ Endocrine (hormone) system

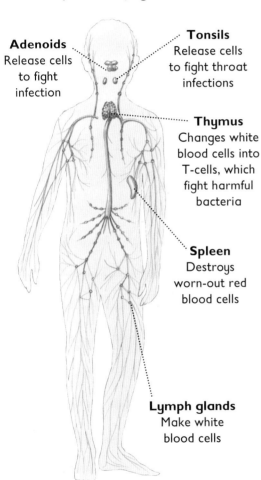

Adenoids
Release cells to fight infection

Tonsils
Release cells to fight throat infections

Thymus
Changes white blood cells into T-cells, which fight harmful bacteria

Spleen
Destroys worn-out red blood cells

Lymph glands
Make white blood cells

Location

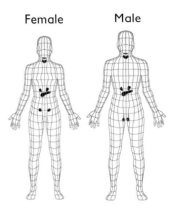

Female   Male

Male and female bodies have the same hormone glands apart from the reproductive parts – ovaries (female) and testes (male).

▼ Lymph gland

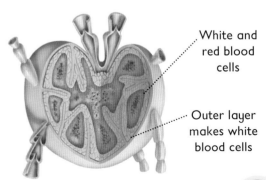

White and red blood cells

Outer layer makes white blood cells

Transport

Cars

Early cars

Benz carriage
Developed by Karl Benz

Model T Ford
Developed by Henry Ford

Lanchester
Developed by
Frederick Lanchester

▼ **New York police car**

▼ **London taxicab**

▲ People carrier

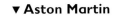

◄ Ferrari

▼ Sir Malcolm
Campbell's *Bluebird*

▲ Racing car

Inside a car

Electrical system
Powers the lights,
temperature gauge
and fuel gauge

Ignition system
Creates an electrical
spark to ignite the fuel

Engine
Burns fuel to
power the car

**Gears in the
gearbox**
Change the speed
that the engine
turns the wheels

Cooling system
Circulates water to prevent
the engine overheating

Car transmission
Takes power from the
engine through the
gearbox to the wheels

Steering gear
Controls the direction
of the car by turning
the front wheels

Brakes
Slow the wheels down
to stop the car

▼ Four-stroke cycle of a petrol engine

Four cylinders give each of these strokes at different times.

1. Inlet valve opens

2. Piston falls, which sucks in the air and fuel mixture

3. Inlet valve closes

4. Piston rises, which squeezes the fuel

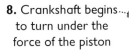

5. Spark plug ignites the fuel

6. The fuel and air mixture expands

8. Crankshaft begins to turn under the force of the piston

7. The gases force the piston down

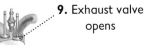

9. Exhaust valve opens

11. Crankcraft continues to turn and the whole process begins again

10. Piston rises, pushing out the burned gases

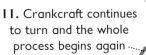

Suspension
Keeps the wheels in contact with the road

Bikes

▼ Bicycle

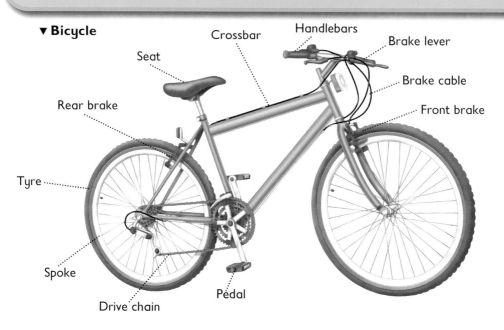

- Seat
- Crossbar
- Handlebars
- Brake lever
- Brake cable
- Front brake
- Rear brake
- Tyre
- Spoke
- Drive chain
- Pedal

▶ Bicycle brakes

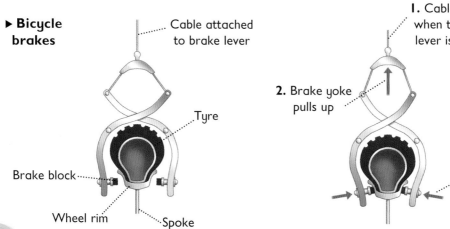

- Cable attached to brake lever
- Tyre
- Brake block
- Wheel rim
- Spoke

1. Cable is pulled when the brake lever is pressed

2. Brake yoke pulls up

3. Brake blocks push against wheel rim, which slows down the movement of the wheel

▶ Penny farthing

▲ Aerodynamic bicycle

◀ Tandem bicycle

◀ Vespa scooter

▼ Motorbike

▲ Racing motorbike

Working machines

▶ **Articulated lorry**

▼ **Cement mixer**

▲ **Tow truck**

◀ **Monster truck**

▲ **Steam roller**

▶ **Excavator**

◀ **Bulldozer**

▼ **Dump truck**

▼ **Scraper**

Working machines

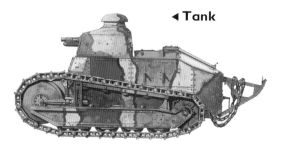

◄ Tank

▲ Fire engine

▼ Tractor and plough

▶ **Combine harvester**

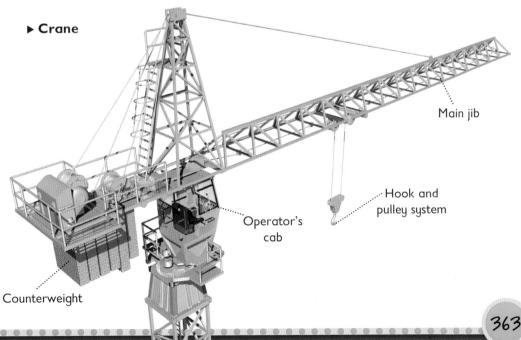

▶ **Crane**

Main jib

Hook and
pulley system

Operator's
cab

Counterweight

Trains

▼ Diesel-electric train

Cooling fan

Diesel engine

Electricity generator

▼ Maglev train

▼ Eurostar

Track
electromagnets

Train
electromagnets

Concrete
T-section track

▲ Big Boy
steam locomotive

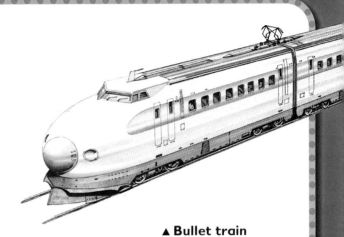

▲ Bullet train

▶ Monorail

Side wheels to
stabilize train

Monorail

Wheels to drive
train forwards

▲ Early US
locomotive

Water transport

◀ **Phoenician ship**

▲ **Chinese junk**

▶ **Viking longship**

▼ **Ancient Greek cargo ship**

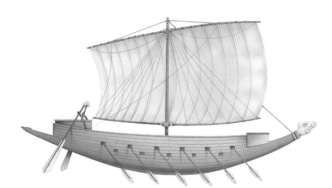

▲ **Egyptian warship**

▼ **SS Great Britain**

▲ **Santa Maria**

▶ **Golden Hind**

▶ **SS Great Eastern**

◀ **Endeavour**

▶ **SS Titanic**

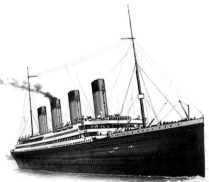

Water transport

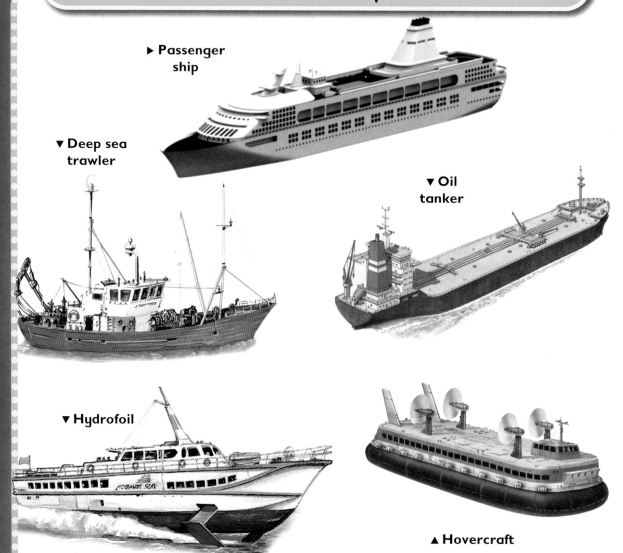

▶ Passenger ship

▼ Deep sea trawler

▼ Oil tanker

▼ Hydrofoil

▲ Hovercraft

Warships

▼ **World War I German U-boat, or submarine**

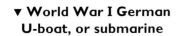

▶ **HMS *Dreadnought***
British World War I
warship

◀ **Q-ship**
British World War I
warship

▼ ***Bismarck***
German World War II
warship

Aircraft

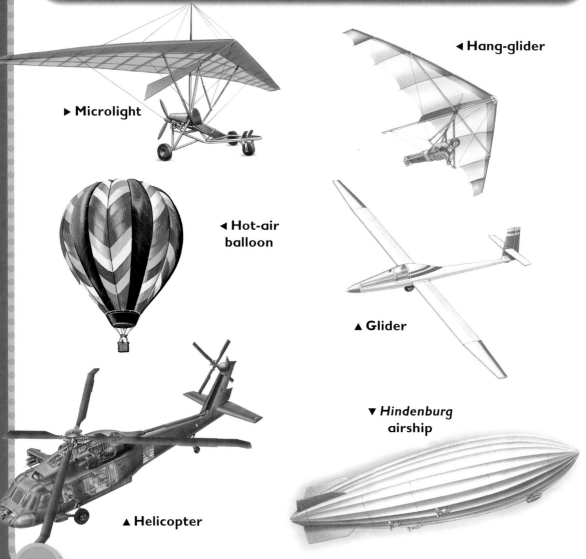

► Microlight

◄ Hang-glider

◄ Hot-air balloon

▲ Glider

▲ Helicopter

▼ *Hindenburg* airship

▼ Hawk jet

▲ Harrier Jump jet

▼ MiG-25
Foxbat

▼ Stealth

▼ Boeing 747
jumbo jet

▼ Concorde

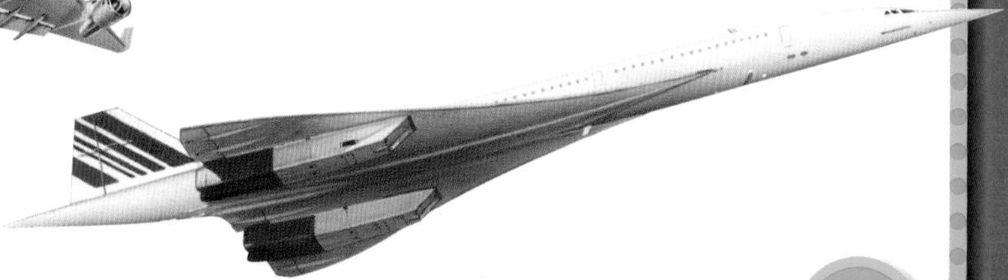

▲ German
Fokker Eindecker

▲ British two-seater
scout aircraft

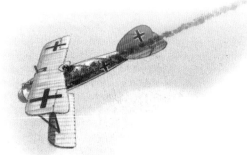

▲ British
Sopwith fighter

▼ German
Albatross

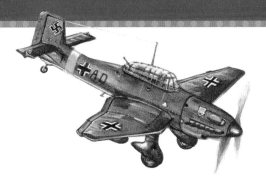

▲ German Junkers 87
dive-bomber

▲ German
Messerschmitt
262

◄ British RAF
Spitfire

◄ British RAF
Avro Lancaster
bomber

Index

Entries in **bold** refer to main subject entries.

Index

Index

Index

Index

Index